AHIMSA

QUEST BOOKS

are published by
The Theosophical Society in America,
a branch of a world organization
dedicated to the promotion of brotherhood and
the encouragement of the study of religion,
philosophy, and science, to the end that man may
better understand himself and his place in
the universe. The Society stands for complete
freedom of individual search and belief.
In the Theosophical Classics Series
well-known occult works are made
available in popular editions.

Cover design by *Marylou Draper*

AHIMSA

(Dynamic Compassion)

By
NATHANIEL ALTMAN

This publication made possible
with the assistance of the Kern Foundation

The Theosophical Publishing House
Wheaton, IL U.S.A.
Madras, India/London, England

This is an original Quest book, published by
The Theosophical Publishing House,
a department of The Theosophical Society in America.

Inquiries for permission to reproduce all,
or portions of this book
should be addressed to:
Quest Books
306 West Geneva Road
Wheaton, Illinois 60187

Library of Congress Cataloging in Publication Data

Main entry under title:
Ahimsa (dynamic compassion)

Bibliography: p.
1. Ahimsa   Altman, Nathaniel, 1948
BJ123.A45A36   291.5   80-51548
ISBN 0-8356-0537-X (pbk.)

Printed in the United States of America

To my mother,

SADIE DAVIS ALTMAN

contents

preface

I first became aware of the term *Ahimsa* when I read some statements by Gandhi in one of my college texts. At the time, the campus was in an uproar over the Vietnam War and I had already experienced my first taste of tear gas and the violent student-police confrontations which took place nearly every day. Amidst all the slogans and political rhetoric, Gandhi's simple approach to life left a deep impression on me.

Although I had been acquainted with the term "non-violence", I had viewed it as a passive term describing the political action of the weak and the helpless. Although the word *Ahimsa* tended to contradict this image, I was suspicious of its exotic Sanskrit origins and felt that Gandhi's philosophy of dynamic harmlessness would be of no lasting practical value here in the West.

However, after exploring the subject with more objectivity, I was impressed by the positive, active meaning of Gandhi's belief in Ahimsa , and was amazed at the wide range of application that Ahimsa can have in the world. Unlike those philosophies which seem to separate one's daily life from the major political and social issues of the day, Ahimsa appeared to encompass every aspect of life; from interpersonal relationships to vast social, political and economic problems; from nuclear disarmament to animal rights; from global environment issues to matters of personal integration and self-realization.

My academic interest in Ahimsa soon began to shift its focus to a more subjective study of the role that Ahimsa could have in my life. Torn by the contradictions between the reality of "what is" and the ideal of "what should be" in my own behavior, I was able to see how my lack of personal integration projected itself onto the world, and how an individual foundation of peace within will naturally enable one to build a peaceful world.

The pathway towards Ahimsa was not as simple as I first believed it to be, although it was also more creative and exciting than I had ever imagined. In the beginning, I seemed to concentrate more on developing the positive outer aspects of Ahimsa in my life at the expense of not coming to terms with the inner factors which caused disharmony in the first place: unresolved conflicts with parents and other authority figures, the desire to escape from the reality of an often violent society, and especially the refusal to see how my subtle greed, dishonesty, and cruelty could affect everyone I meet during the course of the day. I subconsciously feared that if these negative aspects were ever acknowledged and exposed, I would be devastated and my life would be ruined.

It was even more difficult to become aware of how my negative currents would use the ideal of Ahimsa to make me feel superior to others, and "above" many of the problems facing humanity. Also, I was not aware of how I would impose my nonviolent beliefs on others in a way that would be aggressive, manipulative, and self-serving.

Owning up to these realities was a difficult process, and was a major blow to my pride. I had to admit where and how I was not in truth, and especially, I had to be aware of the injury I was causing to others by my behavior. Although I had imagined earlier that taking responsibility for myself in this way would destroy me, I found that quite the opposite was true, and I experienced a new sensation of relief, lightness, and self-acceptance. This experience gave me the strength to confront other distortions in my life with a greater degree of honesty, humor, and compassion. At that point I began to really grasp the essence of Ahimsa.

Gandhi taught that the two pillars of Ahimsa are truth and compassion. If either of these ingredients is missing, Ahimsa cannot manifest itself in our lives. To the degree that there is any coercion, ego-gratification, or the sense of separateness, the essence of Ahimsa is destroyed. For this reason the true strength of Ahimsa can be found through deep self-awareness, the unfolding of active compassion, and the courage to make mistakes and own up to them. Gandhi wrote that while we may never be able to practice Ahimsa in full, we must try to understand its spirit and do our best to make it a reality in our lives.

The preparation of this volume has been one of the greatest gifts I have ever given to myself, and I hope that it will be a source of knowledge and inspiration to others. Collecting the material and preparing the introductions to the various chapters made it possible for me to come into contact with many unfamiliar areas of Ahimsa and to see their value in daily life. In addition, it was necessary to present the many quotations and the commentary in a way that would be easily understood, stimulating and encouraging to read.

The pathway to Ahimsa involves the most exciting journey a person can experience. It helps us tap our deepest sources of inspiration, truth, and compassion. It helps us understand the essence of patience, of humor, and of sharing the best we have to offer. The pathway helps us become integrated, aware and dynamic human beings who care about the world and want to make it a better place for all its citizens. Most of all, Ahimsa involves a unique process of creativity and enjoyment in living which will be reflected in everything we do.

An ancient sage once taught that the seed of Ahimsa dwells in the heart. Although it may be smaller in size than a grain of barley, it is also greater than the earth and all the heavens. Containing the potential to influence all our thoughts, all our desires, and all our actions, the seed of Ahimsa is waiting to be discovered and permitted to flower in our lives. By responding to the often quiet voice of Ahimsa, we can begin to transform our lives and help to create a new world.

NATHANIEL ALTMAN,
Brooklyn, N.Y.
September, 1980.

acknowledgements

All possible care has been taken to obtain permission from the copyright holders to reprint selections protected by copyright; any errors or omissions are unintentional and will be corrected in future printings upon notifying the author, who wishes to express his gratitude to reprint material from the following sources:

The Book Publishing Company, Summertown, TN 38438 for several excerpts from ...this season's people by Stephen Gaskin; The Nvijivan Trust for passages from the works of M. K. Gandhi; Richard St. Barbe Baker for quotations from Sahara Conquest; George Allen & Unwin for an extract from Albert Schweitzer's Civilization and Ethics; Harper and Row for permission to quote excerpts from Reverence for Live by Albert Schweitzer, © 1969 by Rhena Eckert-Schweitzer, Small is Beautiful by E. F. Schumacher, © 1973 by E. F. Schumacher, and Stride Toward Freedom by Martin Luther King, Jr., © 1958 by Martin Luther King, Jr.; Holt, Rinehart and Winston, Publishers, for quotes from The Anatomy of Human Destructiveness by Erich Fromm. Copyright © 1973 by Erich Fromm, Man For Himself by Erich Fromm. © 1947,

Krishnamurti, © 1972 Krishnamurti Foundation, London; reprinted by permission of Harper and Row Pubs., Inc. I gratefully acknowledge the K & R Foundation, Ojai, California, for a quotation from *1966 U.S.A. Talks* by J. Krishnamurti; Molilal Banarsidass (Delhi) for excerpts from *The Philosophy of Non-Violence* by Acharya Rajaneese; The Westminster Press for a passage from *Religion and Violence: A Primer for White Americans*, by Robert McAffee Brown, © 1973 Robert McAffee Brown; Alfred A. Knopf, Inc and Jonathan Cape, Ltd. for a passage from *The Poverty of Power: Energy and the Economic Crisis* by Barry Commoner; Alfred A. Knopf, Inc. for a quotation from *Make Straight the Way of the Lord* by Lanza del Vasto; Random House, Inc. for a quote from *The Wiscom of China and India*, edited by Lin Yutang and *The Environmental Handbook* edited by Garrett de Bell; Coward, McCann & Geohegan for the passage from *Bioenergetics* by Alexander Lowen. © 1975 Alexander Lowen, M. D.

I wish to thank The Institute for the New Age for passages from *Looking In, Speaking Out*, © 1978 Institute for the New Age; Jonathan Cape, Ltd. for two quotations from *Don't Never Forget* by Briget Brophy; Dharma Publishing, Berkeley, California 94704 U.S.A. and for quotes from *Elegant Sayings* by Nagarjuna © 1978 Dharma Publishing, and *A Gesture of Balance* by Tarthang Tulku. © 1977 Dharma Publishing; Routledge & Kegan Paul Ltd. for the passage from the *Lankavatara Sutra* translated by D. T. Suzuki; Contemporary Books Inc, Chicago, for the quote from *Stevenson*, edited by Grace and David Darling, © 1978.

I wish to express my appreciation to The Rosicrucian Fellowship for the passage from the *Rosicrucian Cosmo-Conception* by Max Heindel; Simon and Schuster for permission to use material from *Einstein on Peace*, edited by Otto Nathan and H. Norman and *Portraits from Memory* by Bertrand Russell. Copyright 1951, 1952, 1953 © 1956 by Bertrand Russell; Schocken Books Inc. for passages from *Principles and Precepts of the Return to the Obvious* by Lanza del Vasto. Copyright 1945 by Editions

The Bahai Publishing Trust gave permission to use the quotation on page 86 by 'Abdu'l-Baha, from *Baha'i other English terms like nonresistance to evil"* and *'Abdu'l-Baha*, copyright 1943, © 1956, 1976 by the National Spiritual Assembly of the Baha'is of the United States; and my grateful appreciation to Joan Baez for permission to quote from her book *Daybreak*, published by the Dial Press; The New York Review of Books for the passage quoted from *Animal Liberation* by Peter Singer, © 1975 by Peter Singer; Houghton Mifflin Company for the excerpt from *Silent Spring* by Rachel Carson © 1962 by Rachel L. Carson.

During the seven years it took to prepare this book, dozens of people were of great help to the author. He would like to express his special appreciation to the following individuals whose support, criticism, inspiration and advice were crucial to the completion of *Ahimsa*: Mildred Aissen, Robert Altman, Sadie Altman, Rukmini Bratnick, John B. S. Coats, Steven Cutler, H. Jay Dinshah, Virginia Dwan, Elaine Egan. Larry Furst, Albert Gani, Judy Gani, Sandra Gizzo, Brian Graff, Barry Guthertz, Charles Philip Hayes, Geoffrey Hodson, Sandra Hodson, Mary Juff, Linda James, Susan Kedgeley, Liis Kuningas, Peter Massey, Victoria Mucie, Richard Payne, Eva Pierrakos, John C. Pierrakos, M.D., Peri Posocco, Isis de Resende, Jerry Rosser, Gloria Schindler, Rosemarie Stewart, Rev. Lyle Young.

part i

ahimsa: the foundations

ahimsa: the foundations

Nature hath given unto man a countenance not terrible and loathy, as unto other brute beasts, but meek and demure, representing the very tokens of love and benevolence. She hath given him amiable eyes, and in them assured marks of the inward mind. She hath ordained him arms to clasp and embrace. She hath given him the wit and understanding to kiss: whereby the very minds hearts of men should be coupled together, even as though they touched each other. Unto man alone she hath given laughing, a token of cheer and gladness. Unto man alone she hath given weeping tears, as it were a pledge or token of meekness and mercy. Yea, she hath given him a voice not threatening and horrible, as unto other brute beasts, but amiable and pleasant. Nature not yet content with all this, she hath given unto man alone the commodity of speech, and reasoning: the which things verily may specially both get and nourish benevolence, so that nothing at all should be done among men by violence...

—Erasmus

1

ahimsa: the god quality within

For thousands of years, people the world over have sought to experience *Ahimsa* as an inherent, living, active expression of the God Within. The term itself (pronounced A-him'suh) comes to us from the Sanskrit, and has long been defined in the east as "non-injury" or "non-killing". When seen in a more positive Western context, it means "dynamic harmlessness" or more properly "dynamic compassion". Such a definition would not only encompass the renunciation of the will to kill or the intention to hurt any living being through hostile thought, word, and deed, but the conscious integration of compassion into every aspect of daily life.

The term *Ahimsa* has long been subject to misinterpretation. In the West, the word "nonviolence" has been used as the equivalent of Ahimsa, and although the two words can be viewed as similar for practical reasons, an important distinction should be made: Ahimsa implies the active expression of dynamic compassion, while the accepted meaning of "nonviolence" denotes merely a passive state of refraining from violence. It is probable that other English terms like "non resistance to evil" and

5

"passive resistance" are intended to convey the positive, dynamic meaning of Ahimsa instead of a passive or negative one.

Many people have preconceived ideas about the true meaning of Ahimsa, and their images and conclusions have stood in the way of its proper understanding and acceptance in the West. For many, Ahimsa is an exotic term which brings to mind the image of a monk sitting on a Himalayan mountaintop—a quiet, isolated existence far removed from the challenges, conflicts, and choices to be made in the day-to-day world. Others, who focus on its image of passivity, have viewed the practice of Ahimsa as an avoidance of taking a stand in the face of danger or evil. Charges of "standing by when your grandmother is being attacked" or "doing nothing while your country is being invaded" are sometimes presented to illustrate this belief.

Ahimsa has also been criticized as being a dogmatic and absolutist doctrine, which allows little flexibility in its application. The image of permitting a swarm of locusts to lay waste to productive cropland in the name of compassion (for the locusts) is one example of this point of view. Closely allied with this image is the belief that an aspirant to a life of Ahimsa is forced to adhere to a specific doctrine imposed by some outer authority—a situation which can only produce conformity, rigidity, and fear.

On the other hand, some critics consider Ahimsa to be a vague, impractical, and highly sentimental philosophy, to be practiced to a limited degree under certain unusual circumstances. The possibility that a normal individual living in New York City or the suburbs of Houston can practice Ahimsa on a daily basis is regarded as a most absurd idea.

Actually, the true significance and scope of Ahimsa is far removed from these considerations. The teachings of Ahimsa represent the essence of reverence for life to be applied in every facet of daily existence, and represents a creative involvement in life and its movement. Far from advocating the adoption of an escapist lifestyle, the true understanding of dynamic compassion encourages us to joyously accept personal responsibility to respect life and further it as much as possible. Ahimsa stresses positive action when one is confronted with evil or danger. It is not defeatist, it is not sentimental, nor does it imply an avoidance of discomfort or pain or even death. Ahimsa can be called the dynamic expression of compassion and truth in some of the most difficult and dangerous situations.

Ahimsa can be manifested in many ways which appear to gravitate toward four major categories:

1. *Dynamic Compassion:* This aspect of Ahimsa is, by far, the most applicable to daily life, and involves not only renouncing violence where it can usually be expressed, but utilizing loving, healing, and unifying action in all areas of endeavor. This would involve:

a. healing instead of causing harm;

b. respecting and furthering life instead of limiting or destroying it;

c. serving as an active channel for compassion by opening the heart.

This aspect of Ahimsa can be expressed on a personal level in our relationship with other people, with other species of animals and plants, towards the environment, and in our participation in politics, economics, and education.

2. *Nonresistance to Evil:* Combating an injustice with active love (known as *agape* in Greek). When applied in the context of a social or political movement, this aspect of Ahimsa involves the practice *satyagraha*, which is translated into English as "soul force" or "truth force". Gandhi believed that truth (*satya*) implies love, and firmness (*agraha*) engenders and, therefore, can serve as a synonym for force. In practical terms, satyagraha would simply mean "holding fast to" or "adherence to" truth. Gandhi was perhaps the foremost exponent of both Ahimsa and satyagraha in this

century, and sought to practice it faithfully in his campaign to secure the independence of India from Great Britain.

In many quarters, satyagraha has been confused with the philosophy of "passive resistance", but there is a marked difference between them. Passive resistance, as commonly understood, implies the action of the weak, unarmed or helpless. It does not reject violence as a matter of principle, but because of the lack of a means to violence. It can even serve as a preparatory stage to acts of armed resistance. The underlying objective is to harass or manipulate the opponent into a desired course of action.

Satyagraha, on the other hand, rejects violence as a matter of principle. The idea is not to harass or destroy the opponent but to convert or win him over by patience, honesty, sympathy, or self-suffering. It believes in the inherent goodness of every human being. An aspirant to satyagraha, Gandhi taught that a *satyagrahi* devotes his/ her life to constructive activities in the spirit of service to humanity, whatever the calling may be. For the person who is dissatisfied with mediocrity, the attributes of honesty, service, and integrity represent viable alternatives in a society where deceit, manipulation and dishonesty are often the rule.

3. *Nonviolent Direct Personal Action:* This aspect of Ahimsa can take the form of peaceful demonstrations, vigils, speaking out for truth and justice, and other active work for peace. The application of this facet of Ahimsa may even involve personal danger, such as protecting another person with one's body during an attack, or risking one's own safety in helping others during an epidemic, fire, rape, or other tragedy.

4. *Noncooperation:* Respectful disobedience to an unjust law or command. Examples of noncooperation can include sit-ins, non-participation in military service, boycotts, strikes, fasts, peaceful occupations of property, or the refusal to pay a tax that would finance war.

Pure intent and common sense are basic aspects of Ahimsa. Since the impact of Ahimsa is directly proportionate to the underlying motive of the individual who seeks to practice it, honest self-confrontation is extremely important. Ulterior motives of ego gratification, manipulation and divisiveness can destroy the fragile essence of Ahimsa, and produce only hollow, confusing, temporary results.

Common sense is also basic to Ahimsa, which demands sound judgment in its application. The practice of Ahimsa should be based on a careful reflection of the matter at hand, weighing all the possibilities and alternatives trying to anticipate the limitations. Only then can the aspirant to Ahimsa make a sensible judgment according to his or her abilities, knowing that a perfectly *Ahimsic* solution may not always be possible. Gandhi wrote that "Ahimsa is the highest duty. Even if we cannot practice it in full, we must try to understand its spirit and refrain as far as humanly possible from violence."

The spirit of Ahimsa is based on the unitive quality of life as evidenced through the realms of Nature. It can be seen in the cooperative structure of the atom; the symbiotic relationship among planets, soil, and air; the social quality among people and other species of animals; and even in the magnetic forces that maintain the balance of the solar system. Magnetism, cooperation, and unity are basic to life, and are fundamental to all growth and development.

Ahimsa can take many forms, and can be integrated and applied into all facets of daily life. Dynamic compassion is not for the few. It is an inherent part in the life of any man, woman, or child; and it is within the reach of everyone who sincerely desires to claim it.

2

ahimsa through the ages

Ahimsa Paramo Dharma
(Ahimsa is the highest duty)
—Padmapurana 1.31.27

The philosophy of Ahimsa is as old as the hills, yet it is always new and creative when put into practice. Although the roots of Ahimsa extend to the Himalayas of India and Nepal, its fruits have been shared throughout the world.

Lord Mahavira

The first lightbearer of Ahimsa was the Lord Mahavira, who lived from 599-527 B.C. As the spiritual father of the Jain religion, his simple message to "regard every living being as thyself and hurt no one" forms the foundation of the Harmless Life. Among his three million modern day followers, some try to practice Ahimsa to an extreme, and have led outsiders to believe that Ahimsa is a doctrine of fanaticism. According to the Jain text *Atma Tatva Vichar:*

11

अहिंसा

A monk has to be overscrupulous to avoid any injury to subtle or gross beings, while moving, talking, eating, drinking, rising, sitting, or sleeping. This is the reason why the monks maintain a broomstick with them. With the help of extremely soft tips of woolen threads of the broom they gently remove any living insect which might crawl on the body, dress, or other utensils lest it might be injured.

Gautama Buddha

Born as Prince Siddhartha, the Gautama Buddha (566-486 B.C.) attained enlightenment in his thirtieth year. Considered by millions as the embodiment of a life of Ahimsa, his Noble Eightfold Path has been a guide to the Harmless Life for thousands of years:

Right Belief	Right Means of Livelihood
Right Thought	Right Exertion
Right Speech	Right Remembrance
Right Action	Right Meditation

The followers of the Buddha are taught to show understanding, forebearance, and brotherly love to all human beings without distinction, as well as an unswerving kindness to other members of the animal kingdom.

In one of his discourses, the Buddha taught:

Him I call a Brahmin who is free from anger, who gladly endures reproach, and even stripes and bonds inflicted upon him without cause. Him I call a Brahmin who slays no living creature, who does not kill or cause to be killed any living thing.

Tao Te King

The *Tao Te King*, although relatively short in length, has left a major impact on early Chinese thought. Written by Lao Tzu, a historian and teacher who was associated with Confucius, the *Tao Te King* has been a clear and reliable guide to human conduct for thousands of years:

Through compassion, one will triumph in attack
and be impregnable in defense. What heaven suc-
cors, it protects with a gift of compassion.

—LXVII:165

In addition to serving as a personal guide for right
living, the *Tao Te King* exhorted both armies and entire
kingdoms to abandon warfare as a means to settle disputes. One of the most moving passages in the *Tao* in-
cludes the following observations:

The Master who is a Captain of Soldiers
Does not give blessings with his weapons.
Soldiers' weapons are hated by most men.
Therefore he who has the Tao gives them no
    place...
He who has killed many men
    should weep with many tears.
He who has conquered in battle
    should stand in the place of mourning.

—XXXI

The Dhammapada

Known as the "Lessons of Doctrine", *The Dhammapada* contains the essence of the Ahimsic teaching of the
Buddha. Unlike some other early texts like the *The Laws
of Manu*, and the *Mahabharata*, *The Dhammapada* specifically and directly applies universal issues from a personal viewpoint, very much like the Buddha would teach
his many disciples as he wandered from town to town.

Enmities do not abate here at any time through
enmity; and they abate through friendliness. This
is the eternal Dharma (law).

I.5

Abstention from abusive words, abstention from
injury, strict adherence to the Law...striving in
higher thoughts: this is the instruction of the
Buddhas (the Enlightened Ones).

XIV:7

13

The Upanishads

The Sanskrit word *Upanishad* means "a sitting, an instruction, the sitting at the feet of a master." Although many spiritual discourses can be rightly called Upanishads—such as the Sermon on the Mount—most of the teachings known by that name were composed between 800-400 B.C., and collected by various individuals over the years.

One of the principal messages of the Upanishads is that the spirit can only be known through union with God and not through ordinary learning or scholarly pursuits. For this reason, many of the Upanishads are poetic and inspirational, and their simple message often transcends the realm of conceptual thought. As a powerful source of the Ahimsic doctrines, the Upanishads teach not "love thy neighbor as thyself" but "thy neighbor *is* thyself".

> And the same thing does the Divine Voice here thunder, repeat Da! Da! Da! That is to be self-controlled, giving and compassionate. One should practice this same triad: self restraint, giving, and compassion.
>
> —*Brihadarangaka V.2.3.*

The Laws of Manu

The Laws of Manu is known as the Vedic text of right living. As one of the ancient books which is now widely available in the West, *The Laws of Manu* offers direct and practical guidance for anyone who seeks to follow the path of Ahimsa. As a direct descendant of *Brahman*, the "imperial, supreme and unrecognizable Principle of the Universe" from which all is created and to which all returns, Manu offers the following guidance to help the student or *chela* lead a life of both joy and responsibility:

> Neither a man who (lives) unrighteously, nor he who (acquires) wealth (by telling) falsehoods, nor

14

he who delights in doing injury, ever attain happiness in this world.

—IV:170

He who does not seek to cause the sufferings of bonds of death to living creatures (but desires) the good of all beings, obtains endless bliss.

—V:46

The Bhagavad-Gita

The Bhagavad-Gita, or "The Lord's Song", is a portion of the Mahabharata, the great epic poem of India. Perhaps the most popular of the early Hindu texts, the *Gita* contains a dialog between Krishna, the Charioteer, and Arjuna, his disciple. Often viewed as a scripture of Yoga, it features the conflict of opposites to help lead Arjuna towards a state of harmony with Divine Law. As an appropriate setting, the dialog takes place on the battlefield of Kurukshetra—the battlefield of the soul. In his sixteenth discourse, Krishna gave Arjuna the following guidance:

Fearlessness, cleanness of life, steadfastness in the Yoga of wisdom, almsgiving, self-restraint and sacrifice and study of the Scriptures, austerity and straightforwardness.

Harmlessness, truth, absence of wrath, renunciation, peacefulness, absence of crookedness, compassion to living beings, uncovetousness, mildness, modesty, absence of fickleness,

Vigor, forgiveness, fortitude, purity, absence of evil and pride—these are his who is born with the divine properties, O Bharata.

—16.1,2,3

The Yoga Sutras of Patanjali

Patanjali is considered the greatest exponent of the science of Yoga, the ancient Hindu philosophy of union with God. Through self-purification, selfless service, discrimination and devotion, the Yoga Sutras, or sacred writings, have been called the basic teachings of many early mystery schools, including the famous Trans Himalayan school to which many Masters of the Wisdom have belonged. Although they were said to have been written down over three hundred years before the birth of Christ, the Yoga Sutras of Patanjali have become extremely popular in the West for their timeless wisdom and practical guidance towards a life of compassion, tenderness and understanding:

> As improper thoughts, emotions (and actions) such as those of violence etc., whether they are done (indulged in) caused to be done or abetted, whether caused by greed, anger or delusion, whether present in mild, medium or intense degree, result in endless pain and ignorance; so there is the necessity of pondering over the opposites.
> —*Sadhana Pada 34*

Holy Bible: the Old Testament Prophets

In the Old Testament, laws are given not only in the book of Leviticus, but through the words and admonishments of many of the prophets. In Isaiah 2:4, we read what this Master of Compassion told the people of Israel, and which today is inscribed on the statue outside the United Nations headquarters in New York City:

> And He shall judge among the nations, and shall rebuke many people: and they shall beat their swords into plowshares, and their spears into pruning hooks: nation shall not lift up sword against nation, neither shall there be war any more.

Jesus the Christ, The New Testament

Many books have been written about Jesus the Christ, and have spoken of his love, compassion and utter humility in the face of danger and death. Although many of Christ's words and deeds have been well documented in

The Bible, His call to the harmless life was the most striking in the Sermon on the Mount:

Blessed are the peacemakers: for they shall be called the children of God.

—Matthew 5.9

Ye have heard that it was said by them of old time. Thou shalt not kill; and whosover shall kill shall be in danger of judgment.

—Matthew 5:21

But I say unto you, that ye resist not evil: but whosoever shall smite thee on the right cheek, turn to him the other also.

—Matthew 5:39

But I say unto you, Love your enemies, bless them that curse you, do good to them that hate you, and pray for them which despitefully use you, and persecute you.

—Matthew 5:44

These concepts are echoed throughout the New Testament as taught not only by Jesus, but by his Apostles. In Paul's Letter to the Romans [12.21] the simple words of Ahimsa say:

Be not overcome of evil
But overcome evil with good.

American Indians

Since these earliest years, Ahimsa has been taught and shared. The bearers of this message, in all cultures, all religions, all teachings bore the fruit of this, one of the earliest traditions of Wisdom. But at times it has leapt from the heart of one of their own culture who attained spiritual insight. For example, the American Indians, having no contact with the rest of the world, evolved a religion of Oneness of all Life, and respect for the lessons of the Great Spirit.

I am Deganawidah, and with the chiefs of the Five
   Nations.
I plant the Tree of the Great Peace...

Roots have spread out from the Tree of the Great
   Peace
the name of these roots is the Great White Roots
   of Peace...

If any man of any nation...shall
   desire to obey the laws of the Great Peace
he may trace the roots to their source and be
   welcome to shelter beneath the Great Peace.

I, Deganawidah, and the chiefs of our Five Nations
   of the Great Peace
we now uproot the tallest pine,
   into the cavity thereby made,
We cast all weapons of war.

Into the depths of the earth,
   into the deep underneath...

We cast all weapons of war.

We bury them from sight forever...
   and we plant again the tree...
Thus shall the Great Peace be established.

The message of Ahimsa has been proclaimed in many
ways by a spectrum of individuals as varied as humanity
itself. But invariably, in every culture and great religion,
there arises this teaching.

Theosophy

With every day, the identity between the animal and
physical man, between the plant and man, and even between the reptile and its nest, the rock, and man—is more
and more clearly shown. The physical and chemical con-
stituents of all being found to be identical, chemical

18

science may well say that there is no difference between the matter which composes the ox, and that which forms man. But the Occult doctrine is far more explicit. It says: Not only the chemical compounds are the same, but the same infinitesimal *invisible Lives* compose the atoms of the bodies of the mountain and the daisy, of man and the ant, of the elephant and of the tree which shelters it from the sum. Each particle—whether you call it organic or inorganic—*is a Life.*

—Helena Petrovna Blavatsky,
The Secret Doctrine, Vol. i, p. 304

3

the voices of ahimsa

We naturally expect that the most prominent voices which speak out for Ahimsa to come from the East. And indeed they do, for the Eastern religions—particularly the Jain, Hindu, and Buddhist—consider Ahimsa to be the law by which to live.

However, there are many other, more varied voices speaking on behalf of the Oneness of all life, on passive resistance, on any of the Ahimsic principles which can be of value in today's world. The founders and early leaders of The Theosophical Society introduced the Eastern Wisdom teachings to the western world in the last century, and brought with these the concept of Universal laws, interdependence of all forms of life, and Ahimsa. The voices of the theosophists eloquently spoke for Ahimsa when it was a new and strange concept to the West.

There are poets (Thoreau) and priests (Daniel Berrigan). There are monks (Thomas Merton) and mystics (Meher Baba); and scientists (Albert Einstein) and activists (Martin Luther King, Jr.), psychiatrists (Erich Fromm) and ecologists (Barry Commoner), all speaking with their own voices, from their own points of view, one truth.

21

Peace Pilgrim, who walks the length and breadth of America, or the Dalai Lama, who has walked the high Himalayas, tell the same Ahimsic story, yet each says it differently. And so it is with Ken Keyes, or Tarthang Tulku, Rajaneesh or Martin Buber. However, the two who said it most nobly left their words indelibly etched in more hearts than any of the others: Dr. Albert Schweitzer and Mohandas K. Gandhi. All of these have spoken so eloquently that it is best to let them speak for themselves —memorably—with voices of Ahimsa.

—1—

Ahimsa, though a negative term, is full of positive meaning, extending from an act of simple kindness to a comprehensive outlook of universal fraternity, and for guiding the search for an adoption of practical steps towards realization of universal brotherhood.

—Chitrabhanu

—2—

Ahimsa, or noninjury, naturally implies nonkilling... Noninjury is not merely nonkilling, however. In its comprehensive meaning noninjury means entire abstinence from causing any pain or harm whatsoever to any living creature, either by thought, word, or deed. Noninjury demands a harmless mind, mouth, and hands. Thus Ahimsa is not mere negative noninjury, it is positive Cosmic Love. It arises from development of the mental attitude in which hatred is replaced by love.

—Geoffrey Hodson

—3—

Ahimsa is soul-force and the soul is imperishable, changeless, and eternal....Our scriptures bear witness that when soul-force is fully awakened in us, it becomes irresistible. But the test and condition of full awakening is that it must permeate every pore of our being and emanate with every breath that we take.

—M. K. Gandhi

—4—

The first law...is "Thou shalt not kill," and that should have the greatest weight with the aspirant to the higher life. We cannot create so much as one particle of dust, therefore what right have we to destroy the very least form?

—Max Heindel

—5—

Q. In what does the chief significance of the doctrine of non-resistance consist?
A. [Non-resistance]...alone makes it possible to tear the evil out by the roots, both out of one's own heart and out of the neighbour's heart. This doctrine forbids doing that by which evil is perpetuated and multiplied. He who attacks another and insults him, engenders in another the sentiment of hatred, the root of all evil. To offend another, because he offended us, for the specious reason of removing an evil, means to repeat the evil deed, both against him and against ourselves—to beget, or at least to free, to encourage, the very demon whom we claim we wish to expell....True non-resistance is the one true resistance to evil. It kills and finally destroys the evil sentiment.

—Leo Tolstoy

—6—

"Reverence for Life," "Surrender of strangeness," "the urge to maintain life"—we hear these expressions around us, and they sound cold and shallow. But even if they are modest words they are rich in meaning. A seed is equally commonplace and insignificant, yet within it rests the germ of a lovely flower or a life-giving food.

—Albert Schweitzer

—7—

Good is all that serves life, evil is all that serves death. Good is reverence for life, all that enhances life, growth, unfolding. Evil is all that stifles life, narrows it down, cuts it into pieces.

—Erich Fromm

—8—

Ethics consist, therefore, in my experience the compulsion to show all will-to-live the same reverence as I do my own. Thus we have given us the basic principle of the moral which is necessary of thought. It is good to maintain and encourage life; it is bad to destroy life or to obstruct it.

—Albert Schweitzer

—9—

The religion of non-violence is not meant merely for the rishis and saints. It is meant for the common people as well.

—M. K. Gandhi

—10—

It is our duty to share and maintain life. Reverence concerning all life is the greatest commandment in its most elementary form. Or expressed in negative terms: "Thou shalt not kill." We take this prohibition so lightly, thoughtlessly plucking a flower, thoughtlessly stepping on a poor insect, thoughtlessly, in terrible blindness because everything takes its revenge, disregarding the suffering and lives of our fellow men, sacrificing them to trivial earthly goals.

—Albert Schweitzer

—11—

Why not declare that there is only one truly dangerous subversion, the subversion of life?...Why not encourage our best brains, scientists, artists, educators, to make suggestions on how to arouse and stimulate love for life as opposed to love for gadgets?

—Erich Fromm

—12—

Ahimsa is not merely nonparticipation in destructive activities; it principally manifests itself in constructive activities—services which lead to the upward growth of man. People say that the Goddess of Ahimsa has very powerful weapons at her command. They are the weapons of love, and are, therefore, creative and not destruc-

24

tive. Yet they do destroy; they destroy hatred, inequality, hunger, and disease.

—Vinoba Bhave

—13—

We are all cells in the body of humanity. Each cell has a specific purpose and function. It is because most cells have not found their purpose and function that they experience painful disharmony within, and the body of humanity is headed for chaos.

—Peace Pilgrim

—14—

Merely passive acquiescence in evil is in no sense to be dignified by the name of nonviolence. It is a travesty of Christian meekness. It is purely and simply the sin of cowardice. Those who imagine that this kind of apathy is nonviolent resistance are doing a great disservice to the cause of truth and confusing heroism with degenerate and apathetic passivity.

—Thomas Merton

—15—

Ahimsa is not the way of the timid or the cowardly. It is the way of the brave ready to face death. He who perishes sword in hand is no doubt brave, but he who faces death without raising his little finger and without flinching is braver.

—M. K. Gandhi

—16—

Non-indulgence in violence alone is not non-violence. Non-violence is much more than that....To awaken non-violence is like becoming a river; getting involved in mere renunciation of violence is like becoming a tank.

—Rajaneesh

—17—

Man cannot claim an instinct for aggressiveness if many of his species show no such instinct and manage to live normal and unfrustrated lives without killing their fellows, hunting, fighting, persecuting minorities, thrashing their wives and dogs or tormenting their children. Indeed, if only one member of the human race displayed no urge to indulge in violent aggression, while being in normal health, it would be enough to disprove the assumption of homo sapiens' ineradicable instinct of violence.

—Jon Wynne-Tyson

—18—

As I proceed in my search for truth it grows upon me that Truth comprehends everything. It is not in *ahimsa* but *ahimsa* is in it. What is perceived by a pure heart and intellect is truth for that moment. Cling to it, and it enables me to reach pure Truth. There is no question there of divided duty. But often enough it is difficult to decide what is *ahimsa*. For instance, the use of disinfectants is *himsa*, and yet we cannot do without it. We have to live a life of *ahimsa* in the midst of a world of *himsa*, and that is possible only if we cling to truth. That is how I deduce *ahimsa* from truth. Out of truth emanates love, tenderness, humility. A votary of truth has to be humble as the dust. His humility increases with the observance of truth.

—M. K. Gandhi

—19—

There is one religion—the religion of love, of heart. There is one message, the message of Ahimsa, the message of beholding one's own Self in all beings.

—Sivananda

part II

ahimsa among people

4

ahimsa and right relationship

Compassion is the very nature and fabric of the
structure of the Universe itself, the characteristic
of its being; for compassion means "feeling with",
and the Universe is an Organism, a vast and
mighty oganism, an organism without bounds,
which may otherwise be called Universal Life-
consciousness.

—G. de Purucker

The earliest teachers of Ahimsa stressed that the quality
of our relationship with each other and the world is primarily related to our level of self-understanding. For that
reason, many who have chosen a path of Ahimsa have
realized the need to develop the more contemplative side
of their nature, and explore the often hidden areas within
where truth, compassion, and wisdom reside. From that
inner source of clarity and strength, it is believed that we
can fully draw upon our wellspring of inspiration and
love, and integrate them into the thoughts, words, and
deeds we project into the outer world. This symbolic
movement of the inflowing tide and the outgoing tide has
long been considered to be essential if we are to live a life
of balance, integration, and poise.

29

The following fragment from a 19th century hymn,
given to us by a utopian religious group known as the
Shakers, reflects this simple idea.

Love the inward, new creation,
Love the glory that it brings;
Love to lay a good foundation
In the line of outward things.

Love a life of true devotion,
Love your lead in outward care;
Love to see all hands in motion,
Love to take your equal share.

—*A Hymn of Love*

Albert Schweitzer, perhaps the most eloquent speaker
for the essence of Ahimsa speaks of that inner growth in
man's conscious in this way: "Reverence for life, which
grows out of a proper understanding of the will to live
contains life—affirmation. It acts to create values that
serve the material, the spiritual, and the ethical development of man."

Perhaps the most troublesome obstacle to a life de-
voted to Ahimsa is the image that our personal power is
minimal and that the quality of our daily life has little
impact on the outer world. Many of us would like to believe that our life is experienced in isolated, watertight
compartments and that the way we conduct our daily
affairs does not have a significant impact on the society in
which we live.

In reality, however, our effect on others is far greater
than many realize. Every day we usually have some form
of contact with between fifty and one hundred people,
whether in the home, at work or school, while shopping
or visiting friends. When seen in this light, a negative
thought, a careless word, or a selfish action can have a
strong potential for causing harm to others. In many
cases, people we encounter may respond to a negative expression, and like a chain reaction, can spread their own
hurtful action to others during the course of the day.
Within a matter of hours, one cruel or thoughtless word
on our part can literally affect hundreds of others, just as
a stone thrown into a pool will affect every molecule of
water in that pool.

Probably most people are the source of perhaps a dozen thoughts, words, or actions which bring about some form of disharmony. When we multiply this by one hundred million or even three billion individuals, we can see how this daily accumulation of disharmony can add to the total store of accumulated disorder in the world. Thus the quality of our relationship contains the seeds for powerful change in the world.

In addition to the more obvious examples of violence, it is important to be aware of the more subtle forms of injury which are often accepted modes of behavior in today's society. The need to avoid gossip, the need to tell the truth, and the need to be aware of possessiveness and jealousy in everyday life and practicing caution against these can help avoid many of the conflicts which plague our everyday existence.

By withholding our feelings from others, we can also be guilty of injury. As with sharing food, the act of sharing feelings can be a source of nourishment to others. A meaningful glance, an embrace, or merely a kind word may be just what the other person needs to make his or her day a more joyous one. When expressed from a place of love and respect, even negative feelings can have a healing effect on others, and are always preferable to holding a grudge. By moving past pride and by communicating with the person directly and honestly, we can be giving of ourselves in the best sense of the word. Very often an angry feeling or negative attitude serves as a mask for a deeper and more powerful attitude or emotion, such as pain, fear, or need.

Respect, loyalty, forgiveness, thoughtfulness, and understanding are all basic components of Ahimsa in relationship, and will unfold naturally as the basic obstacles to Ahimsa are removed. A deep understanding of right relationship in the light of Ahimsa leads to speech which has no thorns and to thoughts and actions which reflect the best we have to offer.

—1—

The world is ourselves, the world is not different from us. What we are we have made the world because we are

31

confused, we are ambitious, we are greedy, seeking power, position, prestige. We are aggressive, brutal, competitive, and we build a society which is equally competitive, brutal, and violent. It seems to me that our responsibility is to understand ourselves first, because *we are* the world.

—J. Krishnamurti

—2—

In our search for a new way, we forget a central spiritual law: that our world, with all of its good and all of its evil, is our creation; that it is a collective expression of our inner selves; that we, in fact, *create our own reality*...Our freedom and our hope as individuals and humanity lies in taking responsibility for the world as our creation and in learning how to change the realms both within and outside of ourselves.

—Wendy Mogey

—3—

If a man foolishly does me wrong, I will return to him the protection of my ungrudging love; the more evil comes from him, the more good shall go from me.

—The Buddha

—4—

Returning hate for hate multiplies hate, adding deeper darkness to a night already devoid of stars. Darkness cannot drive out darkness; only light can do that. Hate multiplies hate, violence multiplies violence, and toughness multiplies toughness in a descending spiral of destruction.

—Martin Luther King, Jr.

—5—

Every little thing is sent for something, and in that thing there should be happiness and the power to make happy. Like the grasses showing tender faces to each other, thus we should do, for this was the wish of the Grandfathers of the World.

—Black Elk

Your countenance, a smile, a simple expression of peace and friendship, small attentions and a sensitivity towards another express a universal language, which is capable of showing us that we humans are much closer to one another than we might imagine.

—Helder Camara

The essence of true religious teaching is that one should serve and befriend all. It is easy enough to be friendly to one's friends. But to befriend the one who regards himself as your enemy is the quintessence of true religion.

—M. K. Gandhi

I have no foes save for those who have not yet had time to be friends. There are no foes who are not friends to be. But I must be a foe to none, or he will be my eventual un-doing, unless in the spirit of the only true agreement—mutual respect amidst gracious difference—I agree with him, my adversary, quickly.

—George S. Arundale

A third reason why we should love our enemies is that love is the only force capable of transforming an enemy into a friend. We never get rid of an enemy by meeting hate with hate; we get rid of the enemy by getting rid of enmity. By its very nature, hate destroys and tears down; by its very nature, love creates and builds up. Love transforms with redemptive power.

—Martin Luther King, Jr.

If you dislike war, respect your neighbor.
And cherish the man who comes from afar.
Venerate the distance in him.
Distance is like an allusion to the infinite.
Love the man in your neighbor.
Love God in the man who comes from afar.

—Lanza del Vasto

The time has come for us to promote our causes graciously and in the spirit of appreciative chivalry towards those whose causes are other than our own. We need each other. We need to respect one another. How little do we tread our own ways as we pour contempt on the ways of others. How much the world and each of us in it need freedom and friendship—to receive and to give.

—George S. Arundale

He who does not attempt to make peace
When small discords arise,
Is like a bee's hive which leaks drops of honey—
Soon, the whole hive collapses.

—Nagarjuna

There is a simple formula for resolving conflicts. It is this: have as your objective the resolving of the conflict, not in gaining of advantage. There is a magic formula for avoiding conflicts. It is this: be concerned that you do not offend, not that you are not offended.

—Peace Pilgrim

But instead of justice, we have seen one thing is at the bottom of all quarrels. In all quarrels you have people screaming at each other "I'M ABSOLUTELY RIGHT!" And the more they are right the more they have the right to knock down their enemies, and to kill them, of course.

—Lanza del Vasto

In all scriptures and in our own experience, impersonal good will, or love, is the universal solvent that dissolves our misconceptions, opens our hearts and minds, or, to use the religious expression, takes away our sins. A person who is non-critical, friendly, and open-minded can be very much aware of the defects in the world, in his fellow beings, and in himself, but instead of judgments he is filled with sympathy, good will, and confidence.

—Alfred Taylor

Each acts upon others inevitably in ways to increase or diminish his own joys and sorrows, depending on whether his action follows the laws of unity which constitute the good and the beautiful, or the ways of separateness which ever cause distortion and conflict.

—N. Sri Ram

—17—

Bad vibrations, like the measles, are contagious. Every time you interact with anger, resentment, or fear you add a little reinforcement to the addictions from which we wish to be liberated. You know the story of the man who bawled out his friend, and the friend went home and fought with his wife, who spanked her child, who then kicked the cat. Now let's turn it around—for good vibrations are also catching. Let's be the man who complimented his friend, and the friend went home and kissed his wife, who was so extra loving to her child that he gave the cat some milk without even being asked!

—Ken Keyes, Jr.

—18—

A thought of hatred does more harm than a blow, for a bruise is swiftly healed, but the power of thought is terrible, and working as it does in finer matter has more powerful results. We swim in a sea of thought, and every thought is purifying or making fouler still that sea.

—Christmas Humphreys

—19—

Ahimsa is not only physical nonviolence, but it is nonviolence in speech and thought. One can harm others by harsh speech or even uncharitable thought, and therefore this is also violence to be abjured. No doubt one always keeps in mind what others have said to him, but does one really bear in mind what one has said to others?

—Chitrabhanu

—20—

To be a conduit for Truth the tongue must never be a flail, a fang, a weather-vane, an acrobat, or a scavenger.

—Mikhail Naimy

अहिंसा

You have to use all your good judgment, all your compassion, and courage, and tact, and taste, to say heavy things to people in ways which will be valuable to them, rather than just knocking them off their own center....You need to be truthful, and you need to be kind. You also need to be helpful, and your information has to be relevant. If you're doing what's right, you'll know it. If not, don't fool yourself.

—Stephen Gaskin

—22—

Compassion is the bridge, the spiritual foundation for peace, harmony, and balance...Once we recognize all that we have in common with others, a feeling of compassion naturally arises and we can no longer treat other people with such indifference. We more easily understand their problems, and as we learn how to heal ourselves, we begin to use our knowledge to help them as well.

—Tarthang Tulku

—23—

What you must do is love your neighbor as yourself. There is no one who knows your many faults better than you! But you love yourself notwithstanding. And so you must love your neighbor, no matter how many faults you see in him.

—Martin Buber

—24—

Live with each other as brothers; for the misery and the trouble of the world are of more importance than all the scientific progress that may be imagined. I conclude by calling upon you by all that humanity holds dear to remember what I say, and whether Christians, Atheists, Jews, Pagans, Heathen, or Theosophists, try to practice Universal Brotherhood, which is the universal duty of all...

—William Quan Judge

Whenever another human being is not experienced as human, the act of destructiveness and cruelty assumes a different quality. A simple example will show this. If a Hindu or a Buddhist, for instance, provided he has a genuine and deep feeling of empathy for all living things, were to see the average modern person kill a fly without the slightest hesitation, he might judge this act as an expression of considerable callousness and destructiveness; but he would be wrong in this judgment. The point is that for many people the fly is simply not experienced as a sentient being and hence is treated as any disturbing "thing" would be; it is not that such people are especially cruel, even though their experience of "living beings" is restricted.

—Erich Fromm

When you are not completely open and truthful to all people—when you are trying to hide a part of your inner feelings—you continue the illusion of separateness from others. Hasn't everyone been caught up in the additions for security, sensation, and power? Are you under the illusion that you have desires and feelings that are so horrible that others will be shocked? Or are we really all one? Deep inside, all of us have experienced this self-imposed suffering and isolation that keeps us from being peaceful and loving—even though we may not have perceived it as self-imposed. We all have been in similar predicaments at one time or another in our lives.

—Ken Keyes, Jr.

We make ourselves to be exactly what we are; and we are, at the same time, our brother's keepers, because each one is responsible for an aeonic chain of causation. There is law in this Universe; things are not ruled by chance; and a man cannot think or speak or act without affecting other beings, to their weal or to their woe.

—George de Purucker

Great elder brothers shall you be, if you will, protecting all younger than yourselves, blessing them with your tender, wise and strong compassion, giving even more as those to whom your compassion is due are more and more behind you on the pathway of Life. Be very tender to little children, yet more tender still to all who err—knowing little of the wisdom; and tenderer still to animals, that they may pass to their next pathway through the door of love rather than through that of hatred. Cherish, too, the flowers and the trees. *You are all of one blood, one source, one goal.* KNOW THIS TRUTH AND LIVE IT.

—*A Message from an Elder Brother*

5

ahimsa: war and peace

> We have the strangest notions of war and peace.
> Practically, we restrict these two words to armed
> conflict, or the absence of it, between one country
> and another. When there is no actual physical
> fighting we say there is peace.
> —George S. Arundale

A noted philosopher once observed that the history of
humanity has been a history of its wars. He noted that
during the past 5,000 years, we have fought over 12,000
wars—approximately two and a half wars each year. With
the passing of the seasons we are witness to at least one
major war between nations, several domestic guerrilla
wars, terrorist attacks, domestic rioting, and other violent manifestations of civil strife.

Despite the slogan that "this war will end all wars,"
most people still accept the idea that violence is a useful
means to settle disputes. In many nations of the world,
war is glorified in textbooks and movies and on televi-
sion; war toys are given to children at Christmastime;
war veterans fondly reminisce about their past experiences; and taxpayers willingly allow the government to

spend a large percentage of their salaries on bombs, planes, and military research.

According to the United Nations, over $8,000 billion (eight trillion dollars) has been spent on armaments since 1900—not including the years of World War II. This sum is equivalent to about $2500 for each person living on earth today, or the lifetime income of the average Indian, Chinese, or Guatemalan.

The planetary expenditure for military development alone has been in excess of $25 billion a year. The United Nations estimates that over 400,000 scientists and engineers—roughly half of the world's total scientific and technical labor force—are now employed in improving existing weapons and in developing new ones. The United States and the Soviet Union together spend two-thirds of the world's military budget, while the remaining one-third is spent by other nations to protect themselves from their neighbors or to maintain order within their own frontiers.

When we consider the subject of war, peace, and international relations, many of us experience frustration over the possible alternatives to war. Some argue over whether or not humanity can be saved. Some maintain that human beings are violent by nature, and the possibility of war is inevitable. Others claim that God, or Nature, played a trick with our development and say we are unable to save ourselves from destruction. Others feel that even though they may desire peace, others do not, so working for peace is an exercise in futility.

Some years ago, Gandhi observed that if hate and violence were the laws of mankind, the human race would have become extinct long ago. Although many of the current problems facing humanity may appear insurmountable, Gandhi's belief in the fundamental wisdom in human nature may be justified. How, then, can the aspirant to Ahimsa deal effectively with the present international situation in a manner that would be lasting and beneficial?

Although the work of peace groups and bodies—such as the United Nations—is very important in working for peace around the world, many have stressed that our first step towards world peace begins with personal transformation. Gandhi believed that if many individuals worked to create peaceful conditions among themselves in daily life, peace among nations would follow as a natural result. Tolstoy stressed that each person develop his or her own political philosophy, and not fall prey to propaganda and other conditioning by the government and other institutions. U Thant encouraged a greater personal understanding of the culture and traditions of people of other lands, which would translate itself into an increased appreciation of their point of view. Albert Einstein and Sir Bertrand Russell urged that the individual learn about the dangers of nuclear war and to translate this understanding into actively campaigning for disarmament. A unique concept of integrating personal and political reality was developed by members of the Political Science Committee of the Institute for the New Age. Their process utilizes role playing, group interaction, simulation and other methods to uncover the specific dynamics of a political issue.

> Political struggles, regardless of how complex or unique they appear, are manifestations of our personal spiritual struggles. We therefore approach each issue by first experiencing our relationships to it. How does the outer conflict reflect an inner conflict that we share? In what ways are the forces blocking resolution a reflection of our own resistance to resolution? What are the operant unconscious motivations that needlessly prolong the conflict? How can these conflicts be resolved on the level of the personality and what do the solutions tell us about resolving political struggles?
> —from *Looking In, Speaking Out*

When a deep personal understanding is reached regarding the issues of world peace, we can discover the proper way of action according to our individual talents, abilities and interests. For a student of Ahimsa, the main focus involves the basic issue that human beings continue to choose the way of armed conflict to settle disputes. Unless we are willing to challenge this pattern on a fundamental level, the cycle of war and its preparation will continue to threaten our existence on this planet.

41

अहिंसा

—1—

The murder of one person is called unrighteous and incurs the death penalty. Following this argument, the murder of ten persons will be ten times as unrighteous and there should be ten death penalties; the murder of a hundred persons will be a hundred times as unrighteous and there should be a hundred death penalties. All the gentlemen of the world know that they should condemn these things, calling them unrighteous. But when it comes to the great unrighteousness of attacking states, they do not know that they should condemn it. On the contrary, they applaud it, calling it righteous.

—Motse

—2—

The world is going mad in mutual extermination; and murder, considered a crime when committed individually, becomes a virtue when it is committed by large numbers. It is the multiplication of their crimes that assures impunity to these assassins.

—Origen

—3—

War has its roots in greed; material ambition has motivated all the nations without exception; all our planning has been directed to the organization of the national life so that material possession, competitive supremacy and individual and national selfish interests would control.

—Alice A. Bailey

—4—

...man in his fatal addiction to war....is not really capable of seeing a constructive alternative to war.

—Thomas Merton

—5—

One who assists the ruler of men by means of the Way does not intimidate the empire by a show of arms. This is something which is liable to rebound.

> Where troops have encamped
> There will brambles grow;

In the wake of a mighty army
Bad harvests follow without fail.
　　　　　　　　　—Lao Tsu

—6—

The choice today is no longer between violence and non-violence. It is either nonviolence or nonexistence.
　　　　　　　　　—Martin Luther King, Jr.

—7—

War with atomic bombs and bacteriological weapons means universal annihilation. Since militarization creates a tendency to decide all problems against the background of a possible war and to indoctrinate the people accordingly, it engenders a mentality that makes impossible the only possible solution.
　　　　　　　　　—Albert Einstein

—8—

Not one of the professed aims of Communism (classless and warless world and the rest) or of the democratic and Christian faith (the sacredness and infinitive worth of every human soul and what-have-you) can be advanced by or salvaged after a nuclear war.
　　　　　　　　　—A. J. Muste

—9—

Here then, is the problem which I present to you, stark and dreadful and inescapable: shall we put an end to the human race; or shall mankind renounce war?
　　　　　　　　　—Bertrand Russell

—10—

The solution of our problems cannot come from science; it can come only from man himself. As long as human beings are systematically trained to commit crimes against mankind, the mentality thus created can only lead to catastrophe again and again. Our only hope lies in refusing any action that may serve the preparation or the purpose of war.
　　　　　　　　　—Albert Einstein

The production of arms is allegedly justified on the grounds that in present-day conditions peace cannot be preserved without an equal balance of armaments. And so, if one country increases its armaments, others feel the need to do the same; and if one country is equipped with nuclear weapons, other countries must produce their own, equally destructive....

And one must bear in mind that, even though the monstrous power of modern weapons acts as a deterrent, it is to be feared that the mere continuance of nuclear tests, undertaken with war in mind, will prove a serious hazard for life on earth.

—Pope John XXIII

—12—

When the citizens of a state are morally weak, to demand that its government be morally strong, is nothing short of sheer stupidity. This would be like calling for the reflection in a mirror to be invariably graceful, when the human visage reflected therein is in itself ugly.

—Chitrabhanu

—13—

War cannot create any real cleavage, even between the people who are fighting against one another. These people seem to be different from one another because they have different minds and bodies, but when judged from the point of view of their souls, all differences are not only secondary but simply false. The spiritual unity of all souls remains inviolable in spite of all wars, and from the point of view of ultimate reality, no soul is really at war with any other soul.

—Meher Baba

—14—

Armies can be reduced and abolished only in opposition to the will, but never by the will, of governments. Armies will only be diminished when people cease to trust governments, and themselves seek salvation from the miseries that oppress them, and seek that safety, not by the complicated and delicate combinations of diplomats, but in the simple fulfillment of that law, binding upon every man, inscribed in all religious teachings, and present in every heart, not to do unto others what you wish them not to do to you—above all, not to slay your neighbors.

—Leo Tolstoy

—15—

I cannot help thinking that in the United Nations we have all classes of musical instruments. We have the economically advanced countries, whose aid is always expected to come with strings. We have the great military powers who represent the brass, and occasionally we have forceful speakers who beat the big drums. Then we have the wind instruments which are capable of playing high and low and also of blowing hot and cold at the same time. Thus we have an orchestra made up of dissimilar instruments, with the responsibility of harmonization falling on the United Nations.

—U Thant

—16—

The time has now come for man's intellect to win out over the brutality, the insanity of war.

—Linus Pauling

—17—

...I am absolutely convinced that peace means action—when necessary revolutionary, but *non-violent*. I recognize that a diseased situation can be brought nearer to health, and therefore nearer to peace, by other means too; but I know that violence, even when directed to good ends, still contains the seeds of death.

—Danilo Dolci

—18—

We have assumed the name of peacemakers, but we have been, by and large, unwilling to pay any significant price. And because we want the peace with half a heart and half a life and will, the war, of course, continues, because the waging of war, by its nature, is total—but the waging of peace, by our own cowardice, is partial.

—Daniel Berrigan

If you have a nation of men who have risen to that height of moral cultivation that will not declare war or carry arms, for they have not so much madness left in their brains, you have a nation of lovers, of benefactors, of true, great, and noble men. Let me know more of that nation; I shall not find them defenseless, with idle hands swinging at their sides. I shall find them men of love, honor and truth; men of an immense industry; men whose very look and voice carry the sentence of honor and shame; and all forces yield to their energy and persuasion. Whenever we see the doctrine of peace embraced by a nation, we may be assured that it will not be one that invites injury; but one, on the contrary, which has a friend in the bottom of the heart of every man, even the violent and the base; one against which no weapon can prosper; one which is looked upon as the asylum of the human race and has the tears and the blessings of mankind.

—Ralph Waldo Emerson

All must realize that there is no hope of putting an end to the building up of armaments, nor of reducing the present stocks, nor, still less, of abolishing them altogether, unless the process is complete and thorough and *unless it proceeds from inner conviction:*...the fundamental principle on which our present peace depends must be replaced by another, which declares that the true and solid peace of nations consists not in equality of arms, but in mutual trust alone.

—Pope John XXIII

Peace imposed by violence is not psychological peace, but a suppressed conflict. It is unstable, for it contains the seeds of its own destruction. The outer condition is not a true reflection of an inner condition. But in peace secured by true nonviolent resistance there is no longer any inner conflict; a new channel is found, in which both the formerly conflicting energies are at work in the same direction and in harmony. Here the outer condition truly reflects the inner condition. This is perhaps one reason why Gandhi called this mode of solving conflict *Satyagra-ha*—"holding to truth". Such a peace endures.

—Richard B. Gregg

—22—

Peace demands the most heroic labor and the most difficult sacrifice. It demands greater heroism than war. It demands greater fidelity to the truth and a much more perfect purity of conscience. The Christian fight for peace is not to be confused with defeatism.

—Thomas Merton

—23—

If you wish to be brothers, let the arms fall from your hands. One cannot love while holding offensive arms. Those armaments, especially those terrible arms which modern society has given you, long before they produced victims and ruins, nourish bad feelings, create nightmares, distrust, and somber resolves; they demand enormous expenditures; they obstruct projects of union and useful collaboration; they falsify the very psychology of peoples.

—Pope Paul VI

—24—

Through these rites a three-fold peace was established. The first peace, which is the most important, is that which comes within the souls of men when they realize their relationship, their oneness, with the universe and all its powers, and when they realize that at the center of the universe dwells *Wakan-Tanka*, and that this center is really everywhere, it is within each of us. This is the real peace, and the others are but reflections of this. The second peace is that which is made between two individuals, and the third is that which is made between two nations. But above all you should understand that there could never be peace between nations until there is first known that true peace which, as I have often said, is within the souls of men.

—Black Elk

6

ahimsa vs. institutionalized himsa

Like its counterpart Ahimsa, the word *Himsa* is a source of confusion among westerners. In the ordinary sense, Himsa is a synonym for the word violence—an overt act of destruction, the exertion of physical force which is meant to affect another, or a type of behavior that is designed to inflict personal injury on people or damage to property. When this type of Himsa is sanctioned by custom or tradition through the institutions of society (such as government, schools, and business), it becomes institutionalized. Warfare between nations is the most obvious form of institutionalized Himsa, which can indeed be classified as institutionalized violence.

However, unlike violence, the word Himsa can be applied to other harmful acts which do not involve physical assault. In the broader sense, Himsa can denote a "violation of personhood" when applied to humans, although it can be expanded to include all other life forms. Whether intentional or unintentional, a *Himsic* act would involve the violation of the unique worth of each individual. When considered in a deeper sense, any act which depersonalizes can be an act of Himsa, because it transforms that person into a mere object to be used and manipulated.

49

अहिंसा

The spectrum of Himsa can be divided roughly into four basic categories:

1. *Personal overt physical assault:* This would include acts of violence such as beating, rape, and murder.

2. *Institutionalized overt physical assault:* Acts of war and police brutality are among the more obvious examples.

3. *Personal covert Himsa:* The psychologically dangerous Himsa where dignity and personhood are denied. Such actions can include hurting another through thought, word, and deed; not giving of oneself when the situation demands it; and individual postures of racism, sexism, prejudice based on age, belief, etc.

4. *Institutionalized covert Himsa:* Where institutions such as business, government, schools, and prisons violate the personhood of society's members. Poor housing, racial discrimination, unemployment, and repressive education fit into this category.

Covert Himsa, either on a personal or an institutionalized level, is especially dangerous because it is often subtle and therefore tolerated within the structure of society itself.

Much of humanity is presently living in a revolutionary situation, where institutionalized Himsa is often accepted as the normal state of affairs. Although there is sufficient land and food technology to easily feed every man, woman, and child on the planet, an average of 15,000 people starve to death every day, while nearly two-thirds of the world's population goes to bed hungry. Twenty percent of the world's people control eighty percent of the earth's resources. War, racism, crime, environment pollution, injustice, and disenfranchisement are among the most obvious manifestations of institutionalized Himsa in society today.

When confronted with this reality, people react in a variety of ways. Some prefer not acknowledge it; others decide to conform to the established order altogether, or try to escape into some kind of spiritualized lifestyle which avoids dealing with government, business and educational institutions as much as possible. On the other hand, there are some people who call for the violent overthrow of those institutions which they feel are responsible for the corruption and evil in the world.

However, many students of Ahimsa see the present situation as a natural result of the failure of human beings to admit their role in the corruption, impersonality, and chaos so evident in modern institutions. They point out that the origins of many institutions were essentially benign and were oriented to serve the real needs of people. When the original intent was corrupted by the lust for wealth and power, tremendous value was given to the outer form of the institution and the human connection seemed to become lost. When that happened, the institution was unable to fully serve the public good, and became a kind of monster without either a conscience or a heart. As business, political, religious, and educational institutions fall into disrepute many people with high ideals refuse to participate in their operation. Those who continue to participate are either subject to the scorn of their neighbors or are often demoralized by the cynical self-serving attitudes of those in charge of the institutions. After a time, such people become disillusioned with their efforts, and so their ability to make moral decisions is often impaired.

The transformation of institutions is a challenging and awesome task. In order to implement fundamental and lasting change people must first challenge their own images and attitudes about government, business, organized religion, and education and so become aware of any distortions which may exist in their own concepts. In some cases it may be necessary to face their own rebellion when it comes to dealing with the "super authority" that institutions often represent. They must also confront their own tendency to psychologically depend on those same institutions by relinquishing their personal responsibility as workers, consumers, citizens, or students.

We need to examine our society and our institutions in more human terms to see how their corruption is related to human weakness and distortions about life. In exploring this often sensitive area, it is useful to observe how the negative aspects of institutions often mirror the negative aspects found in many of us. As an example, take a large bank which willingly lends money to a dictatorial regime and relate that to how we relinquish our ethical values in order to obtain what we want. Like the corrupt politician, do we ever manipulate others to win their support? Consider the preacher who threatens his congregation with hellfire and brimstone and equate that with how we utilize fear in order to gain control over others.

Such critical self-examination is a difficult process because most people would rather not be identified with the traits which we view as destructive to the fabric of society. Some people, particularly, are resistant to this self-examination because they believe that greed, violence, and corruption cannot be transformed either on a personal or an institutional level. Curiously enough, those who have sought to look at these traits more objectively have discovered that they are often distortions of positive aspects which reflect basic human needs: the wish to serve, the quest for union, the principle of growth, the desire to be needed.

When an individual is able to understand the root cause of Himsa on a personal level, it is then possible to begin to transform them into the positive aspects of both personal and institutionalized grace: those of nurturing, selfless service, responsibility, respect, and the desire for equality and justice.

This more profound level of understanding will enable us to go beyond the pseudo-solutions of social and political reform, and concentrate more on the lasting solutions of the problems facing humanity. When viewed from such a perceptive, the role of the citizen, the mystic, the business person, and the politician will take on a more creative and positive meaning, and the possibilities of transforming society through peaceful means are vastly enhanced. From this unique perspective of life intelligence, compassion, and goodwill begin to take their rightful place in the conduct of human affairs.

In the following pages, we will consider some of the more urgent areas of human concern regarding institutionalized Himsa. Some of the writers feel that these concerns are of tremendous importance, and have chosen to express their views about them in a blunt and straightforward way. It should also be noted that like the term *Ahimsa*, the Sanskrit word *Himsa* has no English equivalent, and in some of the following quotes, the word "violence" is sometimes used. I feel that when we speak of injustice, greed, or racism, it is more appropriate to utilize the term *Himsa*, or when applicable, the English words evil, injury, or harm. Hoarding the world's resources or having peasants grow strawberries for export instead of beans for their families may not necessarily be an act of violence, but may well be an act of *Himsa*.

—1—

Hunger, poverty, squalor, privilege, powerlessness, riches, despair, and vicarious living are forms of violence —forms that a society approves and perpetuates. We have been too willing to discuss violence in terms of ghetto uprisings, student unrest, street thievery and thrashing, and have been unwilling to direct our attention to the more pathological types of violence that are acceptable...

—Edward Guinan

—2—

The established, institutionalized violence, this "Violence #1" attracts "Violence #2": the revolt of the oppressed; the revolt of young people who have decided to struggle for a more just and humane world....If we answer violence with violence, the world will get caught up into a spiral of violence. The only practical response is to peacefully but courageously confront those injustices which constitute Violence #1.

—Dom Helder Camara

—3—

It is because of the injustices of our society that the spiral of violence initially gets launched, and until and unless we get at the roots of injustice, we will be dealing in only a superficial way with the problem of violence.

—Robert McAffee Brown

—4—

The violence we want to see restrained is the violence of the hood waiting for us in the subway or the elevator That is reasonable, but it tends to influence us too much. It makes us think that the problem of violence is limited to this very small scale, and it makes us unable to appreciate the far greater problem of the more abstract, more global, more organized presence of violence on a massive and corporate pattern.

—Thomas Merton

—5—

So long as the society was decentralized the chronic violence in city slums and rural areas did not disturb the society as a whole....It is not so much the increase in violence that upsets middle-class Americans as the democratization of violence: the poor and black have become less willing to serve as specialized victims of violence from whites ("legally") and each other (illegally).

—Philip Slater

—6—

If we want to knock the Permissive Society where we might better realize that the problems of an over-populated and polluted world include the moral pollution represented by armies of the mentally ill; the unemployed; old-age pensioners living on the breadline; slums; wars; revolutions; cruelty to children; the vivisection, consumption, and other abuses to tens of millions of sentient creatures; and all the many forms of violence, persecution and exploitation that riddles the entire unregenerate system of mankind. No one who fails to protest actively, and by deed and sacrifice, against the larger obscenity of violence and cruelty and indifference has the right to stand in judgment over the sexual peccadilloes of the bulk of those young people who tend to be lumped under the general heading of The Permissive Society. Equally, neither have the young a sound basis for resenting criticism unless they are prepared to interpret more widely and in a more compassionate sense their slogan "Make Love, Not War".

—Jon Wynne-Tyson

—7—

The key to humanity's trouble...has been to take and not give, to accept and not share, to grasp and not to distribute. This has involved the breaking of a law which has placed humanity in a position of positive guilt. War is the dire penalty which mankind has had to pay for this great sin of separateness.

—Alice A. Bailey

—8—

While developed nations experience unparalleled prosperity, two-thirds of humanity experiences malnutrition which may permanently impair its life expression. The average income of 25 per cent of humanity is more than $1000 a year while more that half of humanity earns less than $100 annually. While there are now sufficient food and technology resources to provide physical security for all humanity, calls for co-operation in international development meet only with polite gestures.

—*Values to Live By*

—9—

The nations which have a wealth of resources are not owners; they are custodians of the world's riches and hold them in trust for their fellowmen. The time will inevitably come when—in the interest of peace and security—the capitalists in the various nations will be forced to realize this and will also be forced to substitute the principle of sharing for the ancient principle (which has hitherto governed them) of greedy grabbing.

—Alice A. Bailey

The technology of *mass production* is inherently violent, ecologically damaging, self-defeating in terms of non-renewable resources, and stultifying for the human person. The technology of *production by the masses*, making use of the best of modern knowledge and experience, is conducive to decentralization, compatible with the laws of ecology, gentle in its use of scarce resources, and designed to serve the human person instead of making him a servant of machines.

—E. F. Schumacher

The new humanity calls for creative statesmanship that will recognize and emphasize this great potential for mankind. It calls for a leadership that is dynamically aware of the essential unity of all human beings, but only through their predestined co-partnership in the Divine Plan for man upon earth, but also by virtue of the fact that they are all living expressions of the one life.

—Meher Baba

A belief in human dignity must be endorsed. This unity must be grasped as something worth fighting and dying for; it must constitute the foundation for all our political, religious and social reorganization and must provide the theme for our educational systems.

—Alice A. Bailey

When people are involved in something constructive, trying to bring about change, they tend to be less violent than those who are not engaged in rebuilding or in anything creative. Non-violence forces one to be creative; it forces any leader to go to the people and get them involved so that they can come forth with new ideas. I think that once people understand the strength of non-violence—the force it generates, the love it creates, the response it brings from the total community—they will not be willing to abandon it easily.

—Cesar Chavez

Once we realize that *ahimsa* has mainly to fear from local and small wars, our task becomes easy and we get the right direction. That sets us to the service of the people around us as we endeavor to see that there is no discord within our field of service. Then we turn our eyes inward, and realize the need for the purification of our minds. This leads us to the right solution of our problems. But if our minds dwell only on the bogey of world wars we do not get down to the root of the matter, but become involved in superficial thinking and external organizations only.

—Vinoba Bhave

There are two powers in the world. The great negative power and the great positive power. One of them is going to win and only one. All those who are using their power against us, to oppress us, to kill our people, to steal our land, to steal our humanity, they're following the way of the great negative power. They cannot win. If we turn to the Creator and continue in the way we are doing here and before we came here (International Non-Governmental Organizations Conference on Discrimination Against Indigenous Populations in the Americas) we cannot lose.

—Art Solomon, A.I.M.

It is the law of love that rules mankind. Had violence, i.e., hate ruled us, we should have become extinct long ago. And yet the tragedy of it is that the so-called civilized men and nations conduct themselves as if the basis of society was violence.

—M. K. Gandhi

7

the soldier of ahimsa

> The discipline essential for a nonviolent soldier
> is of a different kind. The one is to kill; the other to
> die. The one is to hate; the other to love. The one
> is to get angry; the other to remain patient. The
> one is to inspire fear; the other to overcome fear.
> The one is to inflict pain; the other to suffer pain
> without complaint. Although the purpose of train-
> ing the nonviolent soldier is quite different from
> that of training a violent one, both methods of
> training are based upon a study of human psychol-
> logy and its laws.
>
> —R. R. Diwakar

Unlike the traditional soldier who is a product of six or
twelve months of regimentation and military discipline,
the soldier of Ahimsa develops as a result of years of deep
inner exploration and inner discipline. Instead of mind-
lessly following the orders of another, the soldier of
Ahimsa takes personal responsibility for every thought,
word, and action.

As a result of this basic orientation, all outward activities take on a different character and tone. Instead of

causing fear in others, the soldier of Ahimsa seeks to instill confidence and trust. In place of antagonism, the soldier of Ahimsa works to bring about communication and understanding. As opposed to the arrogant self-defense of the traditional soldier, the soldier of Ahimsa is protected by humility and complete vulnerability. In place of contempt for others, the soldier of Ahimsa is full of love and respect.

The practice of Ahimsa is grounded in truth, inner strength, and the courage to take risks. A soldier of Ahimsa is not passive and does not necessarily repress anger or indignation. Christ in His last manifestation as Jesus gave us a model of a soldier of Ahimsa; a person with profound awareness of reality and a total dedication to honesty and truth. In certain situations, such as the time when He overturned the tables and cast the moneychangers out of the temple, the act of Ahimsa included anger and righteous indignation in their honest and clear expression. Like the Christ, the soldier of Ahimsa faces up to and accepts personal responsibility for the true motivation of all thoughts and actions, whatever they may be.

In an extreme case; as when a rabid dog or beserk individual poses a direct threat to the safety of a child, for example, there may be no other alternative to stop such a threat than through violent means when other methods fail. Under these circumstances, the votary of Ahimsa has the responsibility to act in the most harmless manner possible rather than to stand by helplessly and do nothing. However, the motivation behind the action in any situation must be confronted. Is the act motivated by compassion, or is it a result of fear or hatred? The motivation behind any action determines the degree of Ahimsa often more than the outward act itself.

It is also important to understand that Ahimsa is not a type of window dressing. When nonviolence is used as a mere gesture or as a mask to hide a seething violence within, it can be more pernicious than a violent act which is honest and direct. Gandhi once wrote that when nonviolence is used to mask fear or impotence, it is far better to be violent. He believed that there is some hope for the violent, but rarely any hope for the impotent.

The traditional soldier is trained to respond largely to situations which are symptomatic of deeper problems, while the soldier of Ahimsa seeks to deal with the underlying causes of violence and strife. Though an outer situation can serve as a focus and catalyst for action, there lies the deeper task of going beyond the appearance to contact the underlying distortion, misunderstanding or fear which motivates the violent act or destructive attitude. Such a task involves tremendous courage and requires a deep understanding of oneself and others. In this way, the act of "turning the other cheek" takes on a new meaning and commitment.

Many people believe that Ahimsa is a far-off ideal which is beyond the reach of all save for the most exceptional of beings. However since the essence of Ahimsa can be found in every human being, to seek that ideal is an inward quest within the reach of anyone who is truly sincere. As with any form of buried treasure, Ahimsa lies beneath the soil of the human personality including one's fears, distortions, and character traits which inhibit true understanding. For those who are sincere, courageous, and patient, the essence of Ahimsa can be discovered and be integrated carefully into one's entire being.

For the individual who aspires to become a soldier of Ahimsa, the paths toward this goal are exciting and varied. Deep study, quiet reflection, prayer, meditation, and other paths to inner awareness are among the more traditional forms of nonviolent training. Certain other techniques, such as group dynamics and psychodrama, have also been introduced to help the individual come into closer contact with the images, fears, and distortions which influence negative thought and outer behavior. It is believed that if one's negative feelings and images can be exposed and challenged in a safe and supportive atmosphere, the purified forms of negative aggression can be perceived and integrated into one's life. In addition, some of the more noble and positive qualities—such as friendliness, curiosity and protectiveness—which are often used to hide negative intent (such as being insincere or nosy and the desire to dominate others) can be liberated, and take on a more genuine quality and form.

अहिंसा

Whatever the path, the soldier of Ahimsa must be aware of the underlying motives which lead to outer action, and take responsibility for even the more subtle aspects of the personality which influence all thought and behavior. Despite the challenge, a soldier of Ahimsa has a deep faith in the innate goodness of every human being (including oneself) and joyfully and patiently orients his/her activities with that belief as the foundation.

—1—

My optimism rests on my belief in the infinitive possibilities of the individual to develop non-violence. The more you develop it in your own being, the more it overwhelms your surroundings and by and by might oversweep the world.

— M. K. Gandhi

—2—

The hardest metal yields to sufficient heat. Even so must the hardest heart melt before sufficiency of the heat of non-violence. And there is no limit to the capacity of non-violence to generate heat.

—M. K. Gandhi

—3—

The nonviolent resister not only refuses to shoot his opponent but he also refuses to hate him. At the center of nonviolence stands the principle of love. The nonviolent resister would contend that in the struggle for human dignity, the oppressed people of the world must not succumb to the temptation of becoming bitter of indulging in hate campaigns. To retaliate in kind would do nothing but intensify the existence of hate in the universe. Along the way of life, someone must have sense enough and morality enough to cut off the chain of hate. This can only be done by projecting the ethic of love to the center of our lives.

—Martin Luther King, Jr.

—4—

Every act of irreverence for life, every act which neglects life, which is indifferent to and wastes life is a step towards the love of death. This choice man must make at every minute. Never were the consequences of the wrong choice as total and as irreversible as they are today. Never was the warning of the Bible so urgent:

"I have put before you life and death, blessing and curse. Choose life, that you and your children may live." (Deut. 30:19)

—Erich Fromm

—5—

Non-conformity, Holy Disobedience, becomes a virtue and indeed a necessity and indispensable measure of spiritual self-preservation, in a day when the impulse to conform, to acquiesce, to go along, is the instrument which is used to subject men to totalitarian rule and involve them in permanent war.

—A. J. Muste

—6—

Not to yield your soul to the conqueror means that you will refuse to do that which your conscience forbids you to do. Suppose the "enemy" were to ask you to rub your nose on the ground or to pull your ears or to go through such humiliating performances, you will not submit to any of these humiliations. But if he robs you of your possessions, you will yield them because as a votary of *ahimsa* you have from the beginning decided that earthly possessions have nothing to do with your soul.

—M. K. Gandhi

—7—

Aye, fight! But not your neighbor. Fight rather all the things that cause you and your neighbor to fight.

—Mikhail Naimy

—8—

Cowardice asks the question, "Is it safe?" Expediency asks the question, "Is it politic?" Vanity asks the question, "Is it popular?" But conscience asks the question "Is it right?" And there comes a time when one must take a position that is neither safe, nor politic, nor popular but he must take it because his conscience tells him that it is right...

—Martin Luther King, Jr.

—9—

The conscientious objector is a revolutionary. In deciding to disobey the law he sacrifices his personal interests to the most important cause of working for the betterment of society. In matters of crucial significance this is often the only way to bring about social progress: this is particularly true when the prevailing balance of power precludes the successful utilization of normal legal and political institutions. It was in this sense that the Fathers of the American Constitution specifically acknowledged the people's right to revolution.

Revolution without the use of violence was the method by which Gandhi brought about the liberation of India. It is my belief that the problem of bringing peace to the world on a supranational basis will be solved only by employing Gandhi's method on a large scale.

—Albert Einstein

—10—

War will disappear only when men shall take no part whatever in violence and hall be ready to suffer every persecution that their abstention will bring them. It is the only way to abolish war.

—Anatole France

—11—

The larger issue is how to stop wars altogether, not this particular war or that particular war....The larger issue is: man has chosen the way of war, conflict. Unless you alter that totally, you will be caught in this question in which the questioner is caught. To alter that totally, completely, you must live peacefully, not killing, either by word or deed.

—J. Krishnamurti

—12—

How are you going to build this practical structure? From the ground up. By studying, learning about, experimenting with every possible alternative to violence on every level. By learning to say..."NO" to killing in general, and "YES" to the brotherhood of man, by starting new institutions which are based on the assumption that murder in any form is ruled out, by making and keeping in touch with nonviolent contacts all over the world, by engaging ourselves in every possible chance in dialogue with people, groups, to try to begin to change the consensus that it's OK to kill.

—Joan Baez

—13—

Part of the superior power of the nonviolent resister seems to lie in the nature of his character.

He must have primarily that disposition best known as love—an interest in people so deep, so determined, and lasting as to be creative; a profound knowledge of or faith in the ultimate possibilities of human nature; a courage based upon a conscious or subconscious realization of the underlying unity of all life and eternal values or eternal life of the human spirit; a strong and deep desire for and love of truth; and a humility which is not cringing or self-deprecatory or timid but is rather a true sense of proportion in regard to people, things, qualities, and ultimate values. These human traits of love, faith, courage, honesty, and humility exist in greater or less strength in every person. By self-training and discipline they can be developed sufficiently to make a good nonviolent "soldier" out of any ordinary human being. Of course, leaders of a nonviolent movement require these qualities to an unusual degree, just as a general requires military qualities more highly developed than those of a common soldier.

—Richard B. Gregg

—14—

If a person has been subjected to repeated attacks, he will erect defenses to their danger in the future. Nations do the same thing with military establishments. In time, both on a personal level as well as on a national one, maintaining defenses maintains the fear of attack, and so one feels justified in further strengthening the defensive position. But defenses also close one in, with the end result that an individual becomes imprisoned behind his own defensive structure.

—Alexander Lowen

The usual way to generate force is to create anger, desire, and fear. But these are dangerous sources of energy because they are blind, whereas the force of love springs from awareness, and does not destroy its own aims. Out of love and the willingness to act, strategies and tactics will be created naturally from the circumstances of the struggle. Thus, the problems of strategy and tactics are of secondary importance.

—Thich Nhat Hanh

Against an angry man let him not in return show anger, let him bless when he is cursed, and let him not utter speech, devoid of truth, scattered at the seven gates.

* * * *

Let him patiently hear hard words, let him not insult anybody, and let him not become anybody's enemy for the sake of this (perishable) body.

—*The Laws of Manu*

Resist not evil: but whosoever shall smite thee on thy right cheek, turn to him the other also.

Love your enemies, bless them that curse you, do good to them that hate you, and pray for them which despitefully use you, and persecute you.

—Matthew 5:34,44

In all such instances, the tendency of nonviolent resistance is to remove fear, anger, and any foreboding or dread of loss or sense of separateness and to replace these with feelings of security, unity, sympathy, and good will. Since fear and anger are elements of cruelty, the removal of fear and anger will tend to reduce cruelty.

—Richard B. Gregg

"You accuse me of this or that thing—well, it's not true. But there is this thing you are not accusing me of and it is true—'' oh, and your enemy will listen. And of course that's the first thing—to be listened to by your enemy. And another occasion to be listened to, is to search if your enemy hasn't one day in the past said something true, done something beautiful. "Oh, and I did that? Ah, yes—" and he will listen!

—Lanza del Vasto

—20—

The phrase "passive resistance" often gives the false impression that this is a sort of "do nothing" method in which the resister quietly and passively accepts evil. But nothing is further from the truth. For while the nonviolent resister is passive in the sense that he is not physically aggressive towards his opponent, his mind and emotions are always active, constantly seeking to persuade his opponent that he is wrong. The method is passive physically, but strongly active spiritually. It is not passive non-resistance to evil, it is active nonviolent resistance to evil.

—Martin Luther King, Jr.

—21—

The practice of non-violence does not merely imply that the devotee himself shall follow the principle, but it goes further, inasmuch as no violence should be committed or condoned. And indifference is a virulent form of violence! Ahimsa, abstinence from any form of killing or harming, will help cultivate an attitude that will be very useful in eliminating warfare and maintaining world peace.

—Chitrabhanu

—22—

Neither violence, anger, nor lust can be made to disappear through suppression alone. These currents do not end through negation and opposition....Non-violence, love, bliss, and God are all positive and concrete. They have their existence. They are not negatives or merely absence of others. They exist in themselves.

—Rajaneesh

—23—

As for widely prevailing individual feelings of frustration and aggression, there, too, it should be possible to find new channels and outlets. One could organize, for instance, name-calling contests, shame-inducing contests, cursing contests. There could be aggressive public dancing, with the dancers wearing ferocious masks. Such things could be done on an international scale. Many other techniques of a like nature can be found.

—Saul K. Padover

—24—

The fifth requisite in our work is patience. You must not yield to despondency, or attempt to hasten the chemical process of dissolution....You need the patience of the husbandman, who, after committing the seed to the earth, does not disturb the soil every day to see whether it is growing.

—Philalethes

—25—

I believe that having a sympathetic heart, a warm heart, a kind heart, is the essence or the most important thing. Irrespective of whether you believe in a religion or not, or no matter what ideology you follow, if you have this... then even such a violent act of killing someone, if it is done with a really good motive, could go beyond the usual level of killing.

—H. H. The Dalai Lama

—26—

It is only by doing the right thing that we get added strength to do right in the future and also acquire the capacity to see what is right....Ahimsa really denotes an attribute and mode of behavior towards all living creatures based on the recognition of the underlying unity of life.... If we understand this principle thoroughly the application of the ideal in our life will become much easier.

—I. K. Taimni

—27—

Then I was standing on the highest mountain of them all, and round about beneath me was the whole hoop of the world. And while I stood there I saw more than I can tell and I understood more than I saw; for I was seeing in the sacred manner the shape of all things in the spirit, and the shape of all shapes as they must live together like one being. And I saw that the sacred hoop of my people was one of many hoops that made one circle, wide as daylight and as starlight, and in the center grew one mighty flowering tree to shelter all the children of one mother and one father. And I saw that it was holy.

—Black Elk

part III

ahimsa and nature

Ever since the teachings of Ahimsa were first given to the world, special emphasis has been placed on our relationship with Nature. Far from being an ethnocentric (human-oriented) concept, Ahimsa has stressed the inter-cooperation of all life in its diversity of outer forms. The idea of the unity of all life has been expressed by many of the world's great teachers, and was shared by many of the native cultures of North America. Among the Sioux, for example, the Earth was seen as a grandmother, and all four-legged, two-legged and winged beings as her grandchildren. The plants, rivers, streams and mountains were also seen as an expression of the Divine, and were therefore treated with an attitude of respect and cooperation.

Among other cultures, however, the relationship with nature was one of conflict. Since many people had to struggle in order to survive, Nature was seen as an adversary which had to be conquered. This attitude produced a split between mankind and Nature which still has not healed. At the present time, many still see Nature as an adversary, which not only needs to be conquered but also to be exploited as quickly as possible. In many parts of the world the land is being ravaged by factories, urbanization, and roads; animals are being slaughtered by the millions for food and sport; the air and water are being fouled by our wastes, and the earth's material resources are being consumed as though they existed in unlimited supply. Ecologists warn that the prevailing belief that the earth can endure unlimited pollution, exploitation, and abuse will jeopardize the future of all life on this planet.

A study of those aspects of Ahimsa which encompass animals and the earth can yield important insights into our future relationship with them. In the following chapters we will explore these often forgotten areas, and consider how we can heal the split which has separated us from Nature and her myriad life forms.

8

ahimsa and other kingdoms

Although human beings eat other animals for food, perform laboratory experiments on them, hunt them for sport, trap them for their fur and use them for entertainment, we rarely pause to consider whether our practices are ethically defensible.

Most people greet the concept of animal liberation with sarcasm and derision. Those who promote the welfare of the other animals are generally regarded as sentimental bleeding hearts or outright crackpots. Since most of us have been taught that "man has dominion over the animals", the idea that species other than our own should have rights sounds most absurd. Nevertheless, a growing number of people have been viewing the plight of other animals with deep concern. Although humans may have needed to kill members of other species in the past, it is maintained that the "kill-or-be-killed" philosophy of life is not only antiquated, but is dangerous in a modern context. In today's world, it is a fact that the fate of one species in an ecosystem eventually can have an impact on the fate of all the others. As more and more animals are being either decimated by human populations or radically increased through unnatural means, the long-term welfare of humanity itself is brought into serious question.

Although other animals cannot reason nor speak the way humans do, this does not give us the right to do with them as we like. Even though our supposed possession of a soul and superior intelligence are used to create an arbitrary dividing line over rights, the fact remains that all animals have the capacity to experience pain and suffering, and in suffering they are our equals.

Most people do not realize the magnitude of the plight of the other animal species. Certain events, such as the slaughter of whales and baby seals, have begun to elicit concern and concrete action. When details of a United States Department of Defense proposal to use 200 beagles to test poisonous gases became public in 1973, the Department received more letters of protest than it had received about the bombing of North Vietnam.

Though human concern for other animals is presently limited towards those animals which elicit positive feelings (purebred puppies, baby seals, and bald eagles as opposed to rodents used in vivisection, crows, or mongrel dogs) more and more people are becoming aware of the total picture of animal suffering. During the past few years a wide spectrum of animal welfare organizations has been established, and many older groups have become more active and broadly based. Some of the more progressive groups have sponsored consciousness-raising workshops designed to help people de-condition themselves of stereotyped ideas and feelings regarding other animals. Terms like "human chauvinism" and "speciesism" (defined by Peter Singer as a prejudice or attitude of bias toward the interests of one's own species and against those of members of another species) have been introduced into our vocabulary. Some excellent books, such as Singer's *Animal Liberation*, have been written to educate the public about many of the aspects of animal suffering and exploitation, and have received wide attention.

During the 1960's, world concern was focused primarily on exploring alternatives to war between people, and while these efforts continue, the early 1970's seemed to reflect a growing interest towards halting war on the environment. As a logical extension of this new ecological awareness, the concern about endangered animals brought the little-recognized "inter-species war" between humans and other animals into sharp focus.

The concept of an inter-species war is not a new one. Dr. George S. Arundale, the third President of the Theosophical Society shared his larger view on war when he was asked his opinion of the prospects for the League of Nations in 1926.

> ...A league to abolish war between the human and animal kingdoms, an inter-kingdom war, is far more important than a league to abolish inter-human war. The latter, at least, is more or less a war among equals, among those who can, more or less, fight back. There may be some honour, some dignity, some self-respect, in such a war. But war in which one side is practically omnipotent and the other side practically impotent is no war at all, it is just massacre, just the pitting of mental cunning against weak ignorance.
>
> *—You*

Since the unity and interdependence of all life is now recognized as a fact of Nature, there has been deep concern about the long-term effects of an inter-species war, not just for the animals which are the immediate victims, but for the long-term survival of the human species as well.

Ahimsa may be radical, but it is not fanatic. The primary goal of Ahimsa is to eliminate all injury to other life forms, not just because it is best for *our* conscience, well-being and future, but because it is the animal's earthly right to enjoy a life free of slavery, injury, suffering, and premature death at the hands of the more powerful human species.

This chapter will explore some of the areas of concern to a student of Ahimsa: the use of animals for experimentation, other animals as servile products, their use for human recreation, the "ownership" of other animals, and other fundamental issues of related importance.

We need another and a wiser and perhaps a more mystical concept of animals. Remote from universal nature, and living by complicated artifice, man in civilization surveys the creatures through the glass of his knowledge and sees thereby a feather magnified and the whole image in distortion. We patronize them for their incompleteness, for their tragic fate of having taken form so far below ourselves. And therein we err, we greatly err. For the animal shall not be measured by man. In a world older and more complete, gifted with extension of the senses we have lost or never attained, living by voices we shall never hear. They are not brethren, they are not underlings. They are other nations, caught with ourselves in the net of life and time, fellow prisoners of the splendor and travail of the earth.

—Henry Beston

—2—

The world as a whole is at war with the animal kingdom, as witness flesh-eating, hunting, and so forth. The aftermath of inter-kingdom war is inter-human war; and let us clearly realize that war never ends war, that no League of Nations can ever end war, no treaties, no pacts, no agreements, still less force of any kind. The only way to end war is to determine that there shall be no war *anywhere*, for war anywhere means, sooner or later, war everywhere.

—George S. Arundale

—3—

Animal liberation is the next step on from people liberation. As human animals, we must stop hunting, enslaving and eating our fellows. We are not the only species with a right to life, liberty and the pursuit of happiness.

—Brigid Brophy

—4—

The world stands at a parting of the ways and those who suffer know this with deeply anxious hearts. One way leads to destruction. It is the way of the tolerance of cruelty, if not the active engagement in it. It is the was of hunting for sport, the way of vivisection, the way of killing for self-adornment, the way of killing animals for food, the way of making slaves of animals without thought for their happiness and well-being. This is the way the world has been treading.

The other way leads to salvation. It is the way of harmlessness, the way of the recognition of brotherhood with all creatures, the way of tenderness and compassion, the way of service and not of selfishness.

—George S. Arundale

—5—

All life, I regard, as sacred. And, it seems to me, in ethics we are concerned not alone with mankind, but also with animals.

The ethical ideal, as I understand it, is: Help all life; have sympathy with all life; avoid injuring anything living.

—T. L. Vaswai

—6—

All beings are fond of themselves, they like pleasure, they hate pain, they shun destruction, they like life and want to live long. To all, life is dear; hence their life should be protected.

—Mahavira

—7—

Life is as dear to a mute creature as it is to a man. Compassion and living kindness are the hallmarks of achievement and happiness.

—H. H. The Dalai Lama

—8—

...We have no right to inflict suffering and death on another living creature unless there is some unavoidable necessity for it, and that we ought all of us to feel what a horrible thing it is to cause suffering and death out of mere thoughtlessness. And this conviction has influenced me only more and more strongly with time. I have grown more and more certain that at the bottom of our heart we all think this, and that we fail to acknowledge it and to carry our belief into practice chiefly as sentimentalists, though partly also because we allow our best feelings to

79

get blunted. But I vowed that I would never let my feelings get blunted, and that I would never be afraid of the reproach of sentimentalism.

—Albert Schweitzer

—9—

I still believe that man not having been given the power of creation does not possess the right of destroying the meanest creature that lives. The prerogative of destruction belongs solely to the creator of all that lives.

—M. K. Gandhi

—10—

You think you can stamp on that caterpillar? All right, you've done it. It wasn't difficult. And now, make the caterpillar again.

—Lanza del Vasto

—11—

Complete non-violence is complete absence of ill-will against all that lives. It therefore embraces even subhuman life, not excluding noxious insects and beasts. They have not been created to feed our destructive propensities. If we only knew the mind of the Creator, we should find their proper place in His creation.

—M. K. Gandhi

—12—

To affirm life is to deepen, to make more inward, and to exalt the will-to-live.

At the same time the man who has become a thinking being feels a compulsion to give to every will-to-live the same reverence for life that he gives to his own. He experiences that other life as his own. He accepts as being good: to preserve life, to raise to its highest value life which is capable of development; and as being evil: to destroy life, to injure life, to repress life which is capable of development. This is the absolute, fundamental principle of the moral, and it is a necessity of thought.

—Albert Schweitzer

—13—

Perhaps the time has come to formulate a moral code which would govern our relations with the great creatures of the sea as well as with those on dry land. That this will come to pass is our dearest wish.

If human civilization is going to invade the waters of the earth, then let it be first of all to carry a message of respect—respect for all life.

—Jacques-Yves Cousteau

—14—

Personally, I have decided that I do not want to kill. I see a sheep in the field—let it live; I see a bullock in the field —let it live; I see some other creature—let it live; I do not want to kill for me.

—John B. S. Coats

—15—

For fear of causing terror to living beings, Mahamati, let the Bodhisattva who is disciplining himself to attain compassion, refrain from eating flesh.

—Buddha

—16—

Meat can never be obtained without injury to living creatures, and injury to sentient beings is detrimental to (the attainment of) heavenly bliss; let him therefore shun (the use of) meat.

—*The Laws of Manu*

—17—

A man can live and be healthy without killing animals for food; therefore, if he eats meat, he participates in taking animal life merely for the sake of his appetite. And to act so is immoral.

—Leo Tolstoy

—18—

He who permits (the slaughter of an animal), he who cuts it up, he who kills it, he who buys or sells (meat), he who cooks it, he who serves it up, and he who eats it, (must all be considered as) the slayers (of the animal).

—*The Laws of Manu*

—19—

The demand for vegetarian food will increase our production of the right kind of plant foods. We shall cease to breed pigs and other animals for food, thereby ceasing to be responsible for the horror of slaughter-houses where millions of creatures cry in vain because of man's selfishness. If such concentration camps for slaughtering continue, can peace ever come to earth? Can we escape the responsibility for misery when we are practicing killing every day of our lives by consciously or unconsciously supporting this trade of slaughter? Peace cannot come where Peace is not given.

—Rukmini Devi Arundale

—20—

Is any killing humane? Let us recognize the fact that there is no humane killing. Killing is inhuman. It is the last word in inhumanity.

—K. Sankara Menon

—21—

I don't myself believe that, even when we fulfill our minimum obligation not to cause pain, we have the right to kill animals. I know I would not have the right to kill you, however painlessly, just because I liked your flavour, and I am not in a position to judge that your life is worth more to you than the animal's to it.

—Brigid Brophy

—22—

It is easy to take a stand about a remote issue, but the *speciesist*, like the recist, reveals his true nature when the issue comes nearer home. To protest about bullfighting in Spain or the slaughter of baby seals in Canada while continuing to eat chickens that have spent their lives crammed into cages, or veal from calves that have been deprived of their mothers, their proper diet, and the freedom to lie down with their legs extended, is like denouncing apartheid in South Africa while asking your neighbors not to sell their houses to blacks.

—Peter Singer

—23—

Modern civilization has gone astray: it thinks from the head, not the heart. Animals have become a victim of our "researches" in schools and colleges. We sacrifice animals by testing drugs on them and inoculating them with disease. We inflict tortures on them in order to demonstrate to our students lessons in the laboratory...Think of the cruelties inflicted on the monkeys we export to foreign countries for petty profits!

—T. L. Vaswani

—24—

I have just been through the process of killing the cistudo for the sake of science; but I cannot excuse myself for this murder, and see that such actions are inconsistent with the poetic perception, however they may serve science, and will affect the quality of my observations. I pray that I may walk more innocently and serenely through nature. No reasoning whatever reconciles me to this act. It affects my day injuriously. I have lost some self-respect. I have a murderer's experience to a degree.

—Henry David Thoreau

—25—

...In a universe which embraces all types of life and consciousness and all material forms through which these manifest, nothing which is ethically wrong can ever be scientifically right; that in an integrated cosmos of spirit and matter one law must pervade all levels and all planes. This is the basic principle upon which the whole case against vivisection rests. Cicero summed it up in the four words: "No cruelty is useful".

—M. Beddow Bayly

—26—

Congress and the President need *unbiased* advice. Instead of a "blue-ribbon panel" to subdue public outrage at the failure of the cancer "moonshot", the President should appoint a public science council which should be given a clear mandate to ensure that only scientifically advanced, non-animal-using methods be used and that new such methods not involving live animals be developed with all possible speed, using the same grant and contract mechanisms that are now used to support animal experimentation. The public science council should be authorized to acquire the staff necessary to help execute its mission. It should offer cash incentive awards to scientists or research teams for the development of new non-animal-using research techniques. It should provide training grants, fellowships, career development awards and other educational opportunities in non-animal-using research, as Federal agencies now do for animal experimentation.

—Elenor Seiling

—27—

God put the animals in our keeping and made us responsible for their care and protection. We live together on the same planet. Yet, seeking to escape pain ourselves, we do not hesitate to inflict it on our fellow creatures, without compunction. Sowing pain and death, what do we expect to reap?

—Peter Hoffman

—28—

Hunting involves many terrible Karmic aspects. In murdering a father or mother animal, very likely some young creatures are made orphans, left unprotected in the wilderness. And, often, clumsy hunters only succeed in wounding the creatures; thus escaping immediate destruction, the maimed animals may roam in agony for days upon days, until Death finally supervenes. More misery in trapping: caught in the wicked traps, many creatures actually gnaw off their own paws, to gain the precious freedom!

—Swami Noshervanji

—29—

It is my opinion that hunting for sport is hardly a sport in any just sense. The contestants are not evenly matched. If

84

the hunted were equipped with the same powerful and often expensive weapons as the two-legged hunter, and could be taught to use them, then hunting might be more sportsmanlike. But the animals are not likely to be consulted in the matter or given such a break.

—Saul K. Padover

—30—

It is much more exciting and difficult to "shoot" with a camera than with a gun and I wish that more and more adventurous young men would give up the gun in favour of the camera.

—Pandit Jawaharlal Nehru

—31—

As for the nonsense sometimes talked about the beneficial effect of those field-sports which bring men into contact with the sublimities of nature, I will only repeat what I have elsewhere said on the subject, that "the dynamiters who cross the ocean to blow up an English town might on this principle justify the object of their journey by the assertion that the sea-voyage brought them into contact with the exalting and ennobling influence of the Atlantic".

—Henry S. Salt

—32—

Birds are given wings to fly, and they were not created in order to be shut up in tiny cages, where they scarcely have room to hop about. Those who claim to be fond of them should desire their liberty, and if they are anxious to see them and learn more of their habits they can do this by going in for bird observation or "hunting" them with cameras instead of nets and guns. We hope the day will soon come when these beautiful creatures will no more be confined behind bars, but will be free to enjoy the liberty which their Creator gave them.

—W. A. Holmes-Gore

—33—

I care not much for a man's religion whose dog and cat are not the better for it.

—Abraham Lincoln

अहिंसा

—34—

Educate the children in their infancy in such a way that they may become exceedingly kind and merciful to the animals. If an animal is sick they should endeavor to cure it; if it is hungry, they should feed it; if it is thirsty, they should satisfy its thirst; if it is tired, they should give it rest.

—'Abdu'l-Bahá

—35—

1. Thou shalt not whip nor beat domestic animals.
2. Thou shalt not intentionally or carelessly crush beneath thy feet ants and insects.
3. Thou shalt not climb trees to take nests and destroy the eggs.
4. Thou shalt not take delight in fishhooks or arrows in order to get amusement.
5. Thou shalt not catch birds or animals in snares or nets.
6. Thou shalt not alarm and scare away birds sitting in their nests.

—T. L. Vaswani

9

ahimsa and the environment

Praised be you, my Lord, for Brother Wind,
And for the air—cloudy and serene—and every
kind of weather,
By which you give sustenance to your creatures.

Praised be you, my Lord, for Brother Fire,
By whom you light the night,
And he is beautiful and jocund and robust and
strong.

Praised be you, my Lord, for our sister Mother
Earth,
Who sustains and governs us,
And produces various fruits with colored flowers
and herbs.

—St. Francis

Within the past few years, the increasing awareness of air,
water, and land pollution has brought the issue of ecology
—the study of the relationship between living beings and
their environment—into sharp focus. Although much has
been said about ecology (the term itself has become a
household word) surprisingly few people really take it

seriously. Despite the fact that the 1970's were hailed as "The Survival Decade", few substantial changes have actually taken place on a global scale involving the issues of environmental pollution, the proper use and conservation of natural resources, and the development of an energy technology that will provide a source of power that would be both reliable and safe.

Ecologists point out that although a growing awareness of environmental issues is important, many people seem more committed to the *idea* of ecology rather than its *substance*. They warn that the next decade will require a much deeper level of personal commitment to environmental issues than in the past. An article in *Greenpeace Chronicles* expressed this need in simple terms:

> The industrialized world, under capitalism and state communism alike, has made no serious effort to shift away from its criminal waste of resources, its continued dependency on technological systems as unstable as they are gigantic, and its fundamental indifference to the fates of other species of animals and plants.

Perhaps a major obstacle to a deep personal commitment toward solving these issues involves a rather popularized and superficial understanding of the basic issues of ecology itself. In an age of space probes to Saturn and climate-controlled shopping malls, few people understand that ecology contains a revolutionary concept so well understood by early Amerindian cultures: Unlike the long-accepted belief which insists on the exclusive dignity of humans and their independent superiority, dominion, and license to subjugate the Earth, ecology teaches simply that humans are not the center of life on this planet. It stresses that not only are we tied to Nature, but we are *part* of Nature.

Through the study of ecology, we have slowly begun to understand the great systems of order which underlie and carefully guide the complex flow of life on this planet. To the surprise of many pragmatic observers, this quest has taken us far beyond the bounds of scientific thought and into deep mystical understanding. Like religion, ecology seeks to reveal the ancient mysteries of life, and can help us chart a course of evolution which will ensure a future for all of the Earth's inhabitants. By making use of logic, deduction, intuition, and observation, ecology may prove to be the first true science/religion. Albert Schweitzer wrote movingly of this possibility many years ago:

> The deeper we look into nature, the more we recognize that it is full of life, and the more profoundly we know that all life is a secret and that we are united with all life that is in nature. Man can no longer live his life for himself alone. We realize that all life is valuable and that we are united to all this life. From this knowledge comes our spiritual relationship to the universe.

One of the primary laws of ecology teaches that every living thing has a reason for being here, a mission to accomplish, and has been given a special function in the scheme of things. The earliest teachings of Ahimsa—like those of modern ecology—have taught that the Earth is *one body* and that every living thing is part of the whole. If this "body" is to survive, we must learn to respect it, and in turn strive to love and respect all forms of life with which we share this planetary system.

Ecology teaches that all life is interrelated and interdependent, and that each living thing depends on another for insuring its survival. Grass, for example, provides nourishment for millions of tiny invertebrates, which in turn are food for insects. The insects are eaten by frogs and small snakes, which provide nourishment for birds. The birds are eaten in turn by larger mammals and birds. When the larger animals die, they provide food for other living things, and as they decompose, they fertilize the soil on which grass is grown. When this "food chain" is disrupted, the very fiber of life on this planet is affected. As with a house of cards, the removal of one card can bring about the collapse of the entire structure.

During the past hundred years, mankind has been proceeding to destroy the planet at an accelerated pace. As a result of our dream to achieve what is termed a "high standard of living," we have sought to accumulate as many material possessions as possible: two cars in every garage, a plethora of electrical appliances, and a staggering amount of disposable products and packaging. In order to satisfy this dream, many new and larger industries were developed and these industries—as well as many of the products they produce—have been primary consumers of the earth's resources and are the major agents of destruction of the land, water, and air.

Closely related to the issue of ecology is that of energy—the force in Nature which animates all things. In addition to the primary direct energy we receive from the sun, energy is indirectly obtained from plants, from moving air (wind) and from the moving water found in rivers. Energy can be produced through the combustion of certain materials, by the combination of one substance with another (such as the reaction of light cells with the sun's rays) or by the breaking down of elements as in nuclear fission. Some forms of energy are in unlimited supply (solar) while others (coal, oil, water, and uranium) are available in limited amounts or are not equally distributed throughout the planet for general use.

At the present time, the global consumption of energy is enormous, and the demand for energy is increasing dramatically each year. Bearing in mind that some seventy percent of the world's population resides in the so-called "developing " nations, the need for energy is expected to increase sharply by the end of this century. This demand will be all the more acute since many of those living in the "Third World" demand a standard of living which resembles that presently enjoyed by those living in the highly industrialized nations.

In addition to the social alienation and the environmental problems that a high level of material wealth has produced, the continuing demand for limited resources of energy has produced serious political problems. Since coal, water, and petroleum are either in short supply or are not evenly distributed among nations, only those countries who have enough political or economic power may utilize them. Although the production of nuclear energy may not be subject to an inherent scarcity of primary resources, the production of nuclear power is highly centralized, and can easily be manipulated by a small number of individuals or nations in order to achieve their political or economic goals. In addition to the possibility of nuclear accident and a power plant's vulnerability to terrorist attack or natural disaster, safe methods to dispose of nuclear wastes are yet to be developed. For these reasons, the production of nuclear energy poses a genuine threat to the survival of life on this planet.

For a student of Ahimsa, the subject of environment and energy is fundamental, because it is closely linked with every aspect of reverence for life. However, in order to understand environmental issues on a deep level and to work towards lasting solutions, our personal feelings must be explored. When viewed in the context that our inner creations produce the outer reality, how can we explain our lack of harmony with our environment? Does the present environmental/energy crisis reflect the spiritual crisis that afflicts much of humanity today? Can the lack of satisfying relationships produce the need to accumulate unlimited material goods?

As we explore environmental issues from this deeper, more personal perspective, many outer problems will be seen in a new light which will lead to a more energetic, focused and compassionate commitment. When this occurs in an organic way, both individuals and nations will begin to work to establish environmental policies which will address themselves to the long-term survival of the planet and the well-being of all its children.

—1—

God is essence in his very nature; that is to say, that goodness which is natural is God. He is the ground, his is the substance, he is very essence or nature, and he is the true Father and the true Mother of natures.

—Julian of Norwich

Nature must be viewed humanely to be viewed at all; that is, her scenes must be associated with humane affections, such as are associated with one's native place, for instance. She is most significant to a lover. A lover of Nature is preeminently a lover of man. If I have no friend, what is Nature to me? She ceases to be morally significant.

—Henry David Thoreau

—3—

Wilderness is a bench mark, a touchstone. In wilderness, we can see where we have come from, where we are going, and how far we've gone. In wilderness is the only unsullied earth sample of the forces generally at work in the universe.

—Kenneth Brewer

—4—

The earth was created to be loved and inhabited by living, loving, lovable creatures—not industrial robots. Freedom is a magic word—basically it means that Man and every living organism has the right to a healthy habitable earth upon which to life and have water to drink and in which to bathe.

—Richard St. Barbe Baker

—5—

[There is a need to develop an environmental consciousness which] must teach man that there is no natural right to exterminate a form of life; that one is not entitled to desecrate earth, air, water, or space merely because he happens to own, control, or occupy some portion of it; and the fact of "legality" in a human court cannot remove ecological crimes from having planetary implications...

—Robert Bisch

—6—

Reform and development efforts will not achieve their aims if they are not also suffused with an ecological ethic that recognizes the conjugal bond between humankind and the natural world from which there can be no divorce.

—Erik P. Eckholm

—7—

When man imposes his own design on Nature, he interferes with the process of natural selection. The consequences of such interventions cannot be predicted. In his pursuit of short-term gains, man is introducing into the ecosystem a large number of inadequately tested new chemicals, which may have serious and widespread biological implications. Countless living organisms could be affected, including man himself. In the interest of his own comfort in the present, and in the name of progress, man may thus degrade the quality of his own species in the future.

—Mankind at the Turning Point

—8—

The "control of nature" is a phrase conceived in arrogance, born of the Neanderthal age of biology and philosophy, where it was supposed that nature exists for the convenience of man. The concepts and practices of applied entomology for the most part date from that stone age of science. It is our alarming misfortune that so primitive a science has armed itself with the most modern and terrible weapons and that in turning them against the insects it has also turned them against the earth.

—Rachel Carson

—9—

Of the Earth's 30 billion acres, already 9 billion are desert. We look at it this way; plastic surgeons tell us that if a man loses one third of his skin, he dies: he has "had it". As a botanist and arborculturist, I know that if a tree loses one third of its bark it dies. I, therefore, submit that if the Earth loses one third of its green mantle of trees and other healthy vegetation, it, too, will die—the water table will sink beyond recall, and life on this planet will become impossible.

—Richard St. Barbe Baker

Healthy soil is alive—with myriads of helpful bacteria and we must do nothing to destroy them. We must play fair to earth beneath our feet, as we should to the neighbour by our side.

—Richard St. Barbe Baker

To avoid ugliness towards the mineral kingdom is to avoid ugly material forms, forcing the life in this kingdom to look through ugliness upon the outer world. To fashion ugliness in stone, in clay, in steel or iron, or in any other substance belonging to the mineral kingdom is to prostitute that kingdom to ugliness and to make it harder for the life in it to unfold.

—George S. Arundale

To issue fom the workshops of Nature a thing must be worthy of Nature's loving care and most painstaking art. Should it not be worthy of your respect, at least?

—Mikhail Naimy

And in this he showed me something small, no bigger than a hazelnut, lying in the palm of my hand, as it seemed to me, and it was as round as a ball....

In this little thing I saw three properties. The first is that God made it, the second is that God loves it, the third is that God preserves it.

—Julian of Norwich

I Love this Little Weed
A sparkle of life I find in it.
(A lover of nature can find pleasure even in a little growing weed. How much more will a living animal endear itself to him?)
A little weed is growing upon the waist of a wall,
Lovely and Lively.

I water it every day.
It has the importance of Living as it grows.

—Anonymous

—15—

The combined efforts of our contractor, the maintenance staff, and volunteers resulted in completion of the installation of the Hill House septic system. We installed it without damaging the environment. We took up the grassy sod before digging. The limbs were tied out of the way. Ditches were dug by hand so as not to damage the large tree roots. Afterward the sod was replaced and bare areas seeded. I like this new way of working in harmony with surrounding life. It is the manifestation of all our love.

—Rick Day

—16—

Unlike oil or uranium, sunlight is not a commodity to be bought and sold; it cannot be possessed; its value is not inherent but derives from its use—the outcome of its relation to a process; to a task. Solar energy enjoins us to attend to the task; to find the best way to link the task to resources; to cherish the resources that nature lends us, to find value in their social use, rather than profit in their private possession.

—Barry Commoner

—17—

We travel together, passengers on a little spaceship, dependent on its vulnerable resources of air and soil; all committed for our safety to its security and peace; preserved from annihilation only by the care, the work, and I will say, the love we give our fragile craft.

—Adlai Stevenson

ahiṁsā and the environment

95

part IV

the calling

the calling

A life dedicated of Ahimsa brings with it both great challenge and intense joy. Far from involving a superficial or partial goal in life, Ahimsa signifies nothing less than a total personal affirmation of the unity of life, and the conscious desire to co-create with God to build a world where evolution, itegration and compassion are the recognized goals of humanity. It represents our desire to "come home" to our innermost essence where both intelligence and love can guide our lives.

Although a response to the call of Ahimsa will begin a joyous and creative process in our lives, the path also contains many challenges. In our work, we will have to become aware of many of our old images and beliefs and conclusions about ourselves and the world which we have been conditioned to accept since childhood. We will need to become aware of when we separate ourselves from others, and how we view the problems facing humanity as different from our own. We will need to confront the areas in us that are uncaring, lazy, or indifferent and deal with them with courage and decision.

However, since Ahimsa brings with it a greater awareness of our Real Self, we will also begin to recognize other, often neglected aspects of ourselves—our true beauty, our deep compassion, our latent creativity, and our deep yearning for integration with ourselves and the world.

Whether we choose to live in the public eye or devote our energy to activities which are on a more private scale, the active principle of dynamic compassion can fill us with a wellspring of enthusiasm, optimism, and self-esteem which will be seen in our relationships, our study, and our work.

10

ahimsa and inner healing

> If harmlessness is the keynote of your life, you will do more to produce right harmonious conditions in your personality than any amount of discipline along other lines.
>
> —Alice A. Bailey

One of the most challenging and exciting aspects of Ahimsa is that it calls for a high level of personal dedication which is not imposed by an outer authority. Because Ahimsa is based on the premise that it is not an external value but rather a quality found in the core of every human being, Ahimsa offers a unique and positive view of the world which can have a dramatic impact on the life of every individual.

Although the term Ahimsa comes to us from the East, it is clearly allied with the Western traditions of realism, common sense and personal worth and responsibility. Instead of dealing with superficial change, Ahimsa touches the deepest and noblest aspects of human nature. It adheres to the universal law which states that like produces like, order comes out of order, and peace can only be achieved through peace. It maintains that in all situations the ends and the means are one and the same, and that truth, honesty, and compassion must be the foundations for any truly civilized society.

Unlike philosophies which teach that humans are merely the products of their society, Ahimsa maintains that human beings *create* society. Although it is acknowledged that society as a whole can and does influence its individual members, the key to dealing with the problems which confront humanity requires the personal responsibility of each member of that society to work toward their solution. Because we do not live our lives in watertight compartments, our personal thought and behavior in daily life inevitably project onto the whole structure and direction of the world.

A deep understanding of the implications of personal responsibility has the potential of bringing about radical change in our personal lives, which will in turn have an impact on the existing structure of society and its institutions. The economic structure can be realigned so that it serves the common good instead of merely catering to individual and corporate greed. Religion can take on new meaning and value as many of its manmade distortions are exposed and corrected. Instead of frustrating and dehumanizing jobs which enslave millions of people, new systems can be evolved which would rechannel one's creative energies in positive and satisfying ways. Cooperation and unity will prevail over cutthroat competition and alienation. In place of the present educational philosophy which teaches students to conform to the established order of a corrupt and violent society, new orientations can evolve which help the young person develop into an aware, awake, and responsible adult. Even the most important times of our lives—those of birth and deat/—can be viewed in a truly Ahimsic perspective. Birth without violence, and a peaceful, natural, dignified death can be the hallmarks of a new direction in society.

Ahimsa does not involve the idea of "sacrifice in the traditional sense, but concerns itself with relinquishing those images, beliefs and escape mechanisms which cause *dis*-order and *dis*-integration in one's life and the world. As opposed to some teachings which advocate the need for external possessions, stimuli, beliefs in order to be fulfilled, Ahimsa teaches that real happiness lies in the discovery of our deepest and most beautiful qualities—those of true intelligence, justice, and compassion. It is taught that there is no scarcity of these attributes and that they cannot be taken away, but are waiting to be discovered and joyously integrated into our lives. Only by the search within can the essence of Ahimsa be found, and its power, guided by intelligence and compassion, be properly used.

—1—

People ought not to consider so much what they are to do as what they *are*; let them but *be* good and their ways and deeds will shine brightly.

—Meister Eckhart

—2—

With every moral improvement, with every good attribute, every worthwhile subject of study, every good deed, even the smallest, even a goodly conversation, one raises his own spiritual state; and automatically when one part of existence rises to a higher state, all existence is uplifted.

—Abraham Isaac Kook

—3—

We need to honestly observe our daily lives and directly confront our weaknesses and problems. Whether we call this a spiritual path or religion is not important; what matters is that our actions are straightforward and our minds are free from playing games. If we are honest and sincerely love the truth, we can revolutionize our lives.

—Tarthang Tulku

So think as if your every thought were to be etched in fire upon the sky for all and everything to see. For so, in truth, it is.

So speak as if the world entire were but a single ear intent on hearing what you say. And so, in truth, it does.

So do as if your every deed were to recoil upon your heads. And so, in truth, it does.

—Mikhail Naimy

—5—

I never feel that I am inspired unless my body is also. It too spurns a tame and commonplace life. They are fatally mistaken who think, while they strive with their minds, that they must suffer their bodies to stagnate in luxury or sloth. The body is the first proselyte the Soul makes. Our life is but the soul made known by its fruits, the body. The whole duty of man may be expressed in one line, —Make to yourself a perfect body.

—Henry David Thoreau

—6—

To eat well is to take food that strengthens, refreshes and leaves the head clear; food that does not bemuse the intelligence, excite, burn, or weigh on the stomach. It means taking the fruits of the earth you are living on when nature offers them; putting as little space and time as possible between the earth and your mouth; preparing them with the least artifice possible; presenting them raw or cooking them over a gentle heat. It means restoring your health and strength first from the brown bread of the earth, the grey salt of the sea, and olive oil and honey from the sun.

—Lanza del Vasto

—7—

From their earliest possible years, children in homes and in schools greatly need and could most valuably receive counsel and example from parents, teachers, and other associates directly inculcating tenderness and humaneness towards human beings, animals, and all sentient life....A crusade for compassion has already been born and is active to some extent. It gravely needs to be inaugurated on a world scale, chiefly in homes and educational institutions where young people establish their attitudes toward life.

—Geoffrey Hodson

—8—

Everything is virtuous in its nature that fulfills the purpose for which it was ordained; and the better it does this, the more virtuous it is; therefore we call him a good man who leads the contemplative or active life for which his nature fits him; we call the horse good that runs fast and far, which he is created to do; we call the sword good that cuts hard things with ease, for which end it is made.

—Dante

—9—

Right livelihood means that work should not only provide a living but also develop selfhood, foster companionship and nourish the earth. If a business makes money but alienates its members from one another, from themselves and from nature, it is a livelihood—but it is not a right livelihood.

—Mark Gerzon

—10—

A sense of responsibility is the outstanding attribute of those in whom the ''new consciousness'' is awakening. The new consciousness manifests itself as:

Inclusiveness: reflecting a universality of outlook.

Relationship: knowing that all men are one in essence.

Balance: producing clear and unbiased thought.

Realism: accepting facts and things *as they are.*

Initiative: promoting change toward *what ought to be* through acceptance of personal responsibility.

Creativity: transcending personal ambition, the mind is free to receive inspiration and perceive new ideas.

Love of Truth: conceding what while all concepts of truth are ''partial and relative'', truth in daily life involves honesty, fair dealing, and ''right'' relationships.

105

A Sense of Values: realising that the values of the past are inadequate to the quality of human life to be evolved today.

A Sense of Social Justice: realising that the struggle for freedom and equality is the root cause for most social problems in the world.

The Ageless "Virtues": recognizing these as the timeless, fundamental, spiritual basis on which human progress has eventually depended. These include selflessness, love, compassion, duty, generosity, industry or joy in work, trust and trustworthiness, personal integrity, dedication and commitment to group good, and the capacity for steadfast, resolute action.

-World Good Commentary:
Values to Live By

—11—

Make something great of all things. The walk, the drive, the fireside talk, all the household ways, all your earthly obligations, your pleasures and your pains, your strivings and your times of ease—let them be great, the greatest that, so far, has dawned within you—the highest you can reach.

—Geoffrey Hodson

—12—

Let harmlessness, therefore, be the keynote of your life.
1. Harmlessness in thought. This will primarily result in the control of speech.
2. Harmlessness in emotional reaction. This will result in being a channel for the love aspect of the soul.
3. Harmlessness in act. This will produce poise, skill in action and the release of the creative will.

—Alice A. Bailey

—13—

The humanity of the individual—his kindness and compassion toward all created beings—is the real test of civilization. The true barbarian is he who is devoid of humanity. However learned a man may be, whether a master of science, or a paragon of worldly attainment, if he lacks humanity he is still a barbarian.

—Meher Baba

106

For true joy is like the feeling you young people have now. It means letting the noblest and purest thoughts within you inspire your lives. The purest and most beautiful thoughts within us are only those which move us deeply.

—Albert Schweitzer

What shall be my attitude toward other life? It can only be at peace with my attitude towards my own life. If I am a thinking being, I must regard other life than my own with equal reverence. For I shall know that it longs for fullness and development as deeply as I do myself. Therefore, I see that evil is what annihilates, hampers or hinders life. And this holds good whether I regard it physically or spiritually. Goodness, by the same token, is the saving or helping of life, the enabling of whatever life I can influence to attain its highest development.

—Albert Schweitzer

It is in the heart center that our inner nature grows to fullness. Once the heart center opens, all blockages dissolve, and a spirit or intuition spreads throughout our entire body so that our whole being comes alive.

—Tarthang Tulku

An individual who has developed Ahimsa carries about him an invisible aura surcharged with love and compassion even though these may not be expressed at the emotional level. Also, because love is the power which binds together in a spiritual union all the separated fragments of the One Life, any individual who is imbued with such love is inwardly attuned to all living creatures and automatically inspires confidence and love in them.

-I. K. Taimni

So try to visualize all the beings of the world—particularly those who have problems or who are experiencing pain....Free yourself from selfish motivations and transform your problems and emotions into deep compassion towards all beings and all things in nature, so that the entire universe is flooded with compassion. Let this compassion radiate outward from every part of your body, and let us together send our power and energy to all beings so that they may overcome their obstacles and become healthy and happy.

—Tarthang Tulku

—19—

Your Father is the Cosmos.
Your Mother is Nature.
Your brothers are your fellow-men.
Live in harmony with the laws and forces of the Universe, Nature, and of your own being.
Preserve yourself.
Learn the natural and cosmic laws.
Live in peace with yourself, with humanity, with Nature and the Universe.
Live in creative love with and for your fellow-men that they may live for thee.
Peace Be With You.

—*The Essene Code of Life*

NOTES

3

the voices of ahimsa

1. Chitrabhanu; *Jain Master Chitrabhanu Speaks to One World* (Bombay: Divine Knowledge Society), p. 48

2. Altman, Nathaniel; *Eating for Life* (Wheaton: Quest Books, 1977), p. xi

3. Gandhi, M. K.; *All Men Are Brothers* (Ahmedabad: Navajivan Publishing House, 1960), p. 129

4. Heindel, Max; *The Rosicrucian Cosmo-Conception* (Oceanside: The Rosicrucian Fellowship, 1956), p. 460

5. Tolstoy, Leo; *The Kingdom of God is Within You* (New York: The Noonday Press, 1961), pp. 18-19

6. Schweitzer, Albert; *Reverence for Life* (New York: Harper and Row, 1969), p. 119

7. From, Erich; *The Anatomy of Human Destructiveness* (Greenwich CT: Fawcett Publications, 1975), p. 106

8. Schweitzer, Albert; *Civilization and Ethics* (London: George Allen & Unwin, 1961), p. 214

9. Gandhi, M. K.; *Pathway to God* (Ahmedabad: Navajivan Publishing House, 1971), p. 26

10. Schweitzer; *Reverence*, p. 116

11. Fromm, Erich, *War Within Man*; (Philadelphia: American Friends Service Committee, 1963), pp. 28-9

12. Weinberg, A. & L.; *Instead of Violence* (New York: Grossman Publishers, 1963), p. 112

13. Peace Pilgrim; *Peace Pilgrim's Progress* (Cologne, NJ)

14. Merton, Thomas; *The Nonviolent Alternative* (New York: Farrar, Straus & Giroux, Inc., 1980), p. 104

15. Duncan, Ronald, ed.; *Selected Writings of Mahatma Gandhi*; (London: Fontana Books, 1972), p. 58

16. Rajaneesh; *Philosophy of Non-Violence* (Delhi: Motilal Banarsidass, 1968), pp. 17-18

17. Wynne-Tyson, Jon; *The Civilised Alternative*; (London: Centaur Press, 1972), p. 78

18. Iyer, Raghavan N.; *The Moral and Political Thought of Mahatma Gandhi*; (New York: Oxford University Press, 1973), p. 229

19. *Birthday Autograph Book* (Madras: Animal Welfare Board, 1970)

अहिंसा

4

ahimsa and right relationship

1. Krishnamurti, J.; *You Are the World*; (New York: Harper & Row, 1972), p. 42
2. Political Science Committee; *Looking In, Speaking Out* (New York: Institute of the New Age, 1978), p. 10
3. Carus, Paul; *The Gospel of Buddha*; (La Salle, IL: Open Court Publishing Co., 1915), p. 167
4. King, Martin Luther Jr.; *Strength to Love* (New York: Harper and Row, 1963), p. 37
5. Niehardt, John G.; *Black Elk Speaks* (New York: Pocket Books, 1972), p. 163
6. Camara, Helder; *Espiral de Violencia* (Salamanca: Ediciones Sigueme, 1970), p. 56
7. Merton, Thomas, ed.; *Gandhi on Non-Violence* (New York: New Directions Publishing Corp., 1965), p. 67
8. Arundale, George S.; *Peace and War in the Light of Theosophy* (Adyar: The Theosophical Publishing House, 1938), p. 46
9. King, *Strength to Love*, p. 38
10. Lanza del Vasto; *Principles and Precepts of the Return to the Obvious* (New York: Schocken Books, 1974), p. 136

11. Arundale, *Peace and War*, p. 52
12. Nagarjuna; "The Staff of Wisdom" from *Elegant Sayings* (Emeryville, CA: Dharma Publishing, 1977), p. 15
13. Peace Pilgrim; *Steps Toward Inner Peace* (Cologne, NJ: published by the author), p. 33
14. *The Catholic Worker*, January 1977
15. Taylor, Alfred; *A Human Heritage* (Wheaton: Quest Books, 1975), p. 98
16. Sri Ram, N.; *Thoughts for Aspirants*, second series (Adyar: The Theosophical Publishing House, 1973), p. 50
17. Keyes, Ken Jr.; *Handbook to Higher Consciousness*, 5th edition (Berkeley: The Living Love Center, 1975), p. 37
18. Humphreys, Christmas; *Walk On!* (Wheaton, IL: Quest Books, 1971), p. 71
19. Chitrabhanu; *Jain Master Speaks*, p. 48
20. Naimy, Mikhail; *The Book of Mirdad* (Baltimore: Penguin Books, 1971), p. 170
21. Gaskin, Stephen; ...*this season's people* (Summertown, TN: The Book Publishing Company, 1976), p. 62
22. Tulku, Tarthang; *A Gesture of Balance* (Emeryville, CA: Dharma Publishing, 1977), pp. 39-40
23. Buber, Martin; Ten Rungs, *Hasidic Sayings* (New York: Schocken Books, 1947), p. 83
24. Judge, William Q.; *The Heart Doctrine* (Bombay: The Theosophy Company, 1963), p. 69
25. Fromm, *Anatomy*, p. 147
26. Keyes, *Handbook*, p. 33
27. de Purucker, G.; *Golden Precepts* (San Diego: Point Loma Publications Inc., 1971) pp. 102-3
28. *A Message from an Elder Brother* (Adyar: The Theosophical Publishing House), pp. 8-9

5

ahimsa. war and peace

1. Yutang, Lin, ed.; *The Wisdom of China and India* (New York: Modern Library, 1955), p. 793

2. Origen (circa A.D. 185-c. 254)

3. Bailey, Alice A.; *Problems of Humanity* (New York: Lucis Publishing Co., 1964), pp. 38-9

4. Merton, *The Nonviolent Alternative*, p. 67

5. Lau, D. C. trans.; *Tao Te Ching* (Baltimore: Penguin Books, 1963), p. 88

6. King, Martin Luther, Jr.; "Pilgrimage to Nonviolence", *The Christian Century*, 13 April 1960, p. 441

7. Nathan, O. & Norden, H.; *Einstein on Peace* (New York: Simon and Schuster, 1960), p. 466

8. Hentoff, Nat, ed.; *The Essays of A. J. Muste;* (New York: Bobbs-Merrill, 1967), p. 388

9. Russell, Bertrand; *Portraits from Memory* (New York: Simon and Schuster, 1956), p. 235

10. Nathan & Norden, *Einstein on Peace*, p. 104

11. John XXIII; *Pacem in Terris* (Glen Rock, NJ: Paulist Press, 1963), p. 38

12. Chitrabhanu; *Lotus Bloom* (Bombay: Divine Knowledge Society, 1967)
13. Meher Baba; *On War* (Poona: Meher Era Publications, 1972), p. 23
14. Tolstoy, Leo; *On Civil Disobedience* (New York: Signet, 1968), p. 118
15. U. Thant; *Toward World Peace* (S. Brunswick, NJ: Thomas Yoseloff, 1964), p. 371
16. Weinberg, A. & L.; *Instead of Violence* (New York: Grossman, 1963) p. 379
17. Dolci, Danilo; "Non-Violence vs. the Mafia", *Win Magazine*, 15 February 1970
18. Berrigan, Daniel; *No Bars to Manhood* (New York: Doubleday and Company, 1970)
19. Weinberg, *Instead of Violence*, pp. 99-100
20. John XXIII, *Pacem in Terris*, p. 39
21. Gregg, Richard B.; *The Power of Nonviolence* (Nyack, NY: Fellowship Publications, 1959), p. 62
22. Merton, Thomas; *Seeds of Destruction* (New York: Farrar, Strauss & Grioux, 1961), p. 125
23. Kirschner, A & L.; *Blessed are the Peacemakers;* (New York: Popular Library, 1971), p. 113
24. Brown, Joseph, ed.; *The Sacred Pipe* (Norman: University of Oklahoma Press, 1953), p. 115

6

ahimsa vs. institutionalized himsa

1. Guinan, Edward; *Peace and Non Violence*; (New York: Paulist Press, 1973), p. 2
2. Camara, *Espiral de Violencia*, pp. 19, 23, 48
3. Brown, Robert McAffee; *Religion and Violence* (Philadelphia: The Westminster Press, 1973), p. 13
4. Merton, *The Nonviolent Alternative*, pp. 187-8
5. Slater, Philip; *The Pursuit of Loneliness* (Boston: Beacon Press, 1971), p. 30
6. Wynne-Tyson, *The Civilised Alternative*, p. 151
7. Bailey, *Problems of Humanity*, p. 7
8. World Goodwill; *Values to Live By*, October 1973, p. 1
9. Bailey, *Problems of Humanity*, p. 80
10. Schumacher, E. F.; *Small is Beautiful* (New York: Harper and Row, 1973), p. 154
11. Meher Baba, *On War*, p. 43
12. Bailey, *Problems of Humanity*, p. 83
13. Guinan, *Peace and Non Violence*, p. 39
14. Weinberg, *Instead of Violence*, p. 113
15. *Treaty Council News*, p. 27
16. Merton, *Gandhi on Non-Violence*, p. 45

7

the soldier of ahimsa

1. Merton, *Gandhi on Non-Violence*, p. 26
2. Gandhi, M. K., *A Gandhi Anthology*, Book 1 (Ahmedabed: Navajivan Publishing House, 1952), p. 51
3. King, Martin Luther, Jr.; *Stride Toward Freedom* (New York: Harper and Row, 1958), p. 85
4. Fromm, *War Within Man*, pp. 28-9
5. Mayer, Peter, ed.; *The Pacifist Conscience* (Chicago: Henry Regnery Co., 1967), p. 348
6. Merton, *Gandhi on Non-Violence*, pp. 67-8
7. Naimy, *Mirdad*, p. 133
8. *Soul Force*, January 1972
9. Nathan & Norden, *Einstein on Peace*, pp. 542-3
10. Anatole France; *Daily Reading*, December 29
11. Krishnamurti, J.; *Talks By Krishnamurti in the U.S.A. 1966* (Ojai, CA: Krishnamurit Writings, Inc., 1977), p. 40
12. Baez, Joan, *Daybreak* (New York: Dial Press, 1968), pp. 164-5
13. Gregg, *Power of Nonviolence*, p. 49

14. Lowen, Alexander; *Bioenergetics* (Baltimore, Penguin Books, 1975), p. 128

15. Thich Nhat Hanh; "Love in Action", *Fellowship Magazine*, January, 1970

16. Buhler, G., trans.; *The Laws of Manu* (New York: Dover Publications Inc., 1969), p. 314

17. Matthew 6:44

18. Gregg, *Power of Nonviolence*, p. 48

19. *The Catholic Worker*, January, 1977

20. King, *Stride Toward Freedom*, p. 84

21. Chitrabhanu, *Jain Master*, p. 49

22. Rajaneesh, *Non-Violence*, pp. 20, 22

23. Padover, Saul K.; *Aggression Without Weapons* (New York: Ethical Culture Publications, 1968), p. 14

24. Perry, Whiteall, ed.; *A Treasury of Traditional Wisdom* (New York: Simon and Schuster, 1971), p. 380

25. From an address presented at the Theosophical Society Centenary Convention, Adyar, Madras, 21 December 1975.

26. Taimni, I. K.; *The Science of Yoga* (Wheaton, IL: Quest Books, 1967), p. 210

27. Niehardt, John G.; *Black Elk Speaks* (New York: Pocket Books, 1972), p. 36

अहिंसा

8

ahimsa and other kingdoms

1. Beston, Henry; *The Outermost House* (New York: Holt, Rinehart and Winston, Inc., 1977)
2. Arundale, *Peace and War*, p. 29
3. Brophy, Brigid; *Don't Never Forget* (London: Johathan Cape, 1966), p. 19
4. Arundale, George S.; *The Night Bell* (Adyar: The Theosophical Publishing House, 1941), p. 11
5. Vaswani, T. L.; *All Life is Sacred* (Poona: Gangaram Sajandas, 1966), p. 23
6. *Birthday Autograph Book*, January 3
7. Ibid.; July 9
7. Ibid.; July 9
8. Kiernan, Thomas, ed.; *A Treasury of Albert Schweitzer* (New York: Citadel Press, 1965), p. 77
9. Duncan, *Selected Writings*, p. 69
10. Lanza del Vasto, *Principles and Precepts*, p. 136
11. Duncan, *Selected Writings*, p. 134
12. Kiernan, *Treasury*, p. 127

13. Cousteau, Jacques-Yves & Dore, Philippe; *The Whale: Mighty Monarch of the Sea* (Garden City: Doubleday and Company, 1972), p. 256

14. *The Indian Vegetarian Congress Quarterly*, January-March 1977, p. 10

15. Suzuki, D. T., trans.; *Lankavatara Sutra* (London: George Routledge and Sons, 1932), p. 213

16. Buhler, *Manu*, p. 176

17. Tolstoy, *On Civil Disobedience*, p. 128

18. Buhler, *Manu*, p. 176

19. *The Vegetarian Way* (Madras: The Indian Vegetarian Congress, 1967), p. 42

20. *Birthday Autograph Book*

21. Brophy, *Don't Never Forget*, p. 19

22. Singer, Peter; *Animal Liberation* (New York: The New York Review, 1975), pp. 175-6

23. Vaswani, *All Life is Sacred*, p. 29

24. Thoreau, Henry David; *The Heart of Thoreau's Journals* (Boston: Houghton Mifflin Co., 1927), p. 205

25. Bayly, M. B.; *Members of the Theosophical Society and Vivisection* (Letchworth: St. Christopher's Press, 1952), p. 4

26. *Laboratory Animals: Replace Them Now* (United Action for Animals, 205 East 42nd Street, New York, NY 10017 USA)

27. *Birthday Autograph Book*

28. Dinshah, H. J., ed.; *Here's Harmlessness* (Malaga, NJ: The American Vegan Society, 1973), p. 34

29. Padover, *Aggression*, p. 15

30. *Birthday Autograph Book*, December 9

31. Salt, Henry S.; *Animal Rights* (New York: Macmillan, 1894), p. 56

32. Holmes-Gore, V. A.; *These We Have Not Loved* (Rochford, Essex: C. W. Daniel Co., 1971), p. 63

33. *Birthday Autograph Book*, December 2

34. Bahá Ulláh & 'Abdul'l-Bahá; *Bahá'í World Faith* (Wilmette: Bahá'í Publishing Trust, 1956), p. 374

35. Vaswani, *All Life is Sacred*, pp. 126-7

9

ahimsa and the environment

1. Walsh, James, trans.; *Julian of Norwich: Showings* (New York: The Paulist Press, 1978), pp. 302-3
2. Thoreau, *Journals*, p. 139
3. de Bell, Garrett, ed.; *The Environmental Handbook* (New York: Ballantine Books, 1970), p. 148
4. Baker, Richard St. Barbe; *Sahara Conquest* (London: Lutterworth Press, 1966), pp. 168-9
5. Bisch, Robert; *The Ecological Conscience* (Englewood Cliffs, NJ: Prentice-Hall Inc., 1970), p. 13
6. Eckholm, Eric; *Losing Ground* (New York: W. W. Norton & Co., 1976), p. 24
7. Mesarovic, M. & Pestel, E.; *Mankind at the Turning Point* (London: Hutchinson Publishing Group Limited, 1975), p. 15
8. Carson, Rachel; *Silent Spring* (New York: Fawcett Publications, 1962), pp. 261-2
9. Baker, *Sahara Conquest*, p. 173
10. Ibid., p. 175

11. Arundale, George S.; *You* (Wheaton, IL: Quest Books, 1973), p. 45

12. Naimy, *Mirdad*, pp. 170-1

13. Walsh, *Julian of Norwich*, p. 183

14. Vira, Raghu, ed.; *Chinese Poems and Pictures of Ahimsa* (Nagpur: International Academy of Indian Culture, 1954), p. 50

15. *Newsletter of the Center for the Living Force*, September, 1975, p. 22

16. Commoner, Barry; *The Poverty of Power* (New York: Alfred A. Knopf, 1976), p. 165

17. Darling, G. & D. eds.; *Stevenson* (Chicago: Contemporary Books, 1977), p. 4

अहिंसा

10

ahimsa and inner healing

1. Perry, *Treasury*, pp. 346-7
2. Bokser, Ben Zion, ed.; *Abraham Isaac Kook* (New York: Paulist Press, 1978), p. 185
3. Tulku, *Balance*, p. 23
4. Naimy, *Mirdad*, p. 57
5. Thoreau, *Journals*, p. 20
6. Lanza del Vasto, *Make Straight the Way of the Lord* (New York: Alfred A. Knopf, 1974), p. 46
7. Hodson, Geoffrey; *The Call to the Heights* (Wheaton, IL: Quest Books, 1976), pp. 133-4
8. Perry, *Treasury*, p. 335
9. Mark Gerzon in *The New York Times*
10. World Goodwill; *Values to Live By*; October 1973
11. Hodson, Geoffrey; *The Brotherhood of Angels and of Men* (London: The Theosophical Publishing House, 1957), p. 18
12. Bailey, Alice A.; *Treatise on White Magic* (New York: Lucis Publishing Co., 1970), p. 103

13. Meher Baba, *On War*, p. 41
14. Schweitzer, *Reverence for Life*, p. 79
15. Kiernan, *Treasury*, p. 62
16. Tulku, *Balance*, pp. 35-6
17. Taimni, *Yoga*, p. 238
18. Tulku, *Balance*, pp. 43-4
19. Szekeley, Edmond Bordeaux, trans.; *The Essene Code of Life* (International Biogenic Society Apartado 372 Cartago, Costa Rica, Central America), p. 42